BELOW GROUND LEVEL

BELOW GROUND LEVEL

Creating New Spaces for Contemporary Architecture

Ernst von Meijenfeldt

Marit Geluk et al.

Birkhäuser – Publishers for Architecture

Basel · Berlin · Boston

This publication was made possible by the financial support from the Foundation
for the Production and Translation of Dutch Literature

English translation Roz Vatter-Buck

A CIP catalogue record for this title is available from the Library of Congress,
Washington, D.C., USA

Die Deutsche Bibliothek – CIP-Einheitsaufnahme

Below ground level Creating New Spaces For Contemporary Architecture
Ernst von Meijenfeldt, Marit Geluk et al. Transl.: Roz Vatter-Buck.
Basel, Boston, Berlin: Birkhäuser, 2003

© 2003 Birkhäuser – Publishers for Architecture,
P.O.Box 133, CH-4010 Basel, Switzerland for the English edition
A member of the BertelsmannSpringer Publishing Group
Printed on acid-free paper produced from chlorine-free pulp. Printed in Belgium

ISBN 3-7643-6908-6   www.birkhauser.ch

9 8 7 6 5 4 3 2 1

1 Introduction

12 **To be and not to be**

Ernst von Meijenfeldt

14 Underdeveloped

24 **Friedrichstrasse** Berlin

36 **Museumplein** Amsterdam

44 **First green, then grey, then green again**

Interview with Emilio Ambasz

2 Urban Development

52 **The way down is the way out**

Jaap Huisman

56 Impressive

62 **3 km³ Models** Amsterdam

68 **Jubilee Line** London

82 **Manipulation for simultaneity**

Interview with Floris Alkemade

3 Architecture

90 **Subterranean existence**

Jaap Huisman

92 Yawning depths

104 Under fire

108 **Le Carrousel du Louvre** Paris

116 **Villa Hoogerheide** Hilversum

122 **Two withdrawal rooms:**

Glass Temple Kyoto

Souterrain Amsterdam

130 **Tent versus cave**

Interview with Norman Foster

4 Functions

136 **We can get more under ground**

Ernst von Meijenfeldt

and Dick Regenboog

144 No way

146 **Panopticon Prison** Breda

150 **Two restaurants:**

Wagamama London

Restaurant Johan Graz

158 **Rooms and routes set the scene**

Interview with Francine Houben

5 Perception and Cognition

164 **Through a child's eyes**

Diederik Samwel

172 Underexposed

178 The underworld

180 **Itäkeskus swimming pool** Helsinki

186 **Two churches:**

Temppeliaukio church Helsinki

Catedral Metropolitana Brasilia

194 **Beelden aan Zee Museum** Scheveningen

200 **No ostrich policy**

Interview with Jan Benthem

6 Engineering

206 **Reclaiming space from earth and water**

Paul van Deelen

208 The bowels of the earth

218 **Philharmonic Hall** Cologne

224 **Zeeland Archives** Middelburg

230 **Pioneer of the underground**

Interview with John Carmody

7 Energy and Interior Climate

236 **Buildings like icebergs**

Ed Melet

242 The hole in the world

246 **Two housing projects:**

Soft and Hairy House Tsukuba City

Nine Houses Dietikon

256 **Two libraries:**

Law Faculty library Ann Arbor

Marriott Library Salt Lake City

262 **Acknowledgements**

263 **Illustration credits**

264 **Colophon**

Preface

Kees van der Hoeven

Towards the end of my studies, I happened to see two photographs of a house in the woods. The first shows a patio where an older couple is enjoying the sunshine. In the second picture, you can see that this is no ordinary patio, but is rather dug into the woodland. That image hit me right between the eyes... and has stayed with me ever since.

At a glance, I learned that the earth itself could be hollowed out to produce the most beautiful interior and exterior spaces. Later, I also came to understand that even if you are unable to dig very deeply – which is usually the case in my homeland – you can still use the earth to cover buildings.

In the years that followed I have continued to search for examples of beautiful subterranean constructions. Ultimately, I owe my start as a professional to an earth-covered plan. In 1979, after winning a competition calling for ideas for the extension of Berlage's town hall in Usquert, I was hired by the then Dutch government architect, Tjeerd Dijkstra to work as an architect at the Government Buildings Agency. My design covered the planned extension behind the town hall almost entirely with earth and grass, to render its intrusion into the surrounding Groningen countryside as imperceptible as possible.

Back in the 1980s, architect Ernst von Meijenfeldt began intensively investigating subterranean construction, both in his own designs and by collecting inspiring examples during his travels. Therefore, I am delighted that he was chosen by the Centrum Ondergronds Bouwen COB to produce this book on the discovery of underground architecture. He has selected the best examples from the all over the world, documented them with drawings and images, interviewed the designers, and finally grouped the projects around a number of clear themes with accompanying essays.

A proficient architect is very good at three things: combining the many aspects surrounding a design problem into one or more concepts; using his or her imagination to tap into deeper levels of the problem and translate them, in the design, into images that are new to us. Finally, the architect has a good understanding of construction, that complicated process involving so many different parties, regulations and financial calculations.

This book illustrates what happens when inventive architects recognise and make use of the unsuspected architectonic qualities of the space under the familiar surface of the earth. Architectonic quality is seldom created by chance. It results from a process that demands not only professional skill, but also a great deal of energy and love. And that is reflected in this wonderful, lovingly produced book, which I therefore heartily commend to your attention!

Kees van der Hoeven
Chairman of the Royal Institute of Dutch Architects BNA

1 INTRODUCTION

To be and not to be Ernst von Meijenfeldt

Friedrichstrasse Berlin

Museumplein Amsterdam

TO BE AND NOT TO BE

Connection and restraint as themes

Ernst von Meijenfeldt

My fascination with underground architecture, where there is always more than meets the eye, is almost as old as I am. When playing with blocks as a child, I always made buildings with hidden rooms, false floors and foldaway panels. And I was always very interested in the landscape, too, in working the earth. These days, as an architect, I work somewhere in the middle; I look for relationships between buildings and nature and give them form. Traditionally, in the Netherlands, we clear everything away, spray a layer of sand on top and then build on this tabula rasa. *The new on the new, literally detached from God. Building is often about wanting to be seen, concentrating chiefly on the exterior. Building underground, however, means seeking an alliance with the environment, with the landscape. Or at least it can be so, if motives other than functional ones are uppermost. With restraint and introversion as motives, the way leads automatically downwards.*

For me, architecture's task is working with nature, with the landscape, the context. This view is by no means new. If so, then only for architects, since ordinary people have always built this way.

It was in the Greek arts of building, the origin of western architecture, that the process of moving away from nature first became apparent. The close, animistic, intuitive relationship with nature that existed until then made way for one of domination. Man placed himself above nature and was no longer automatically a part of it. In this period, man developed the skill and power of thought, visible in Greek and, later, Roman architecture in the clear, geometric language of form and the importance attached to mathematical proportions. Up until the Renaissance and its associated humanism, architecture was, in a sense, a reflection of the supremacy of man over nature. The original Greek view – that man is the measure of all things – was hard to shake. During that long period

there was a clear distinction between building and architecture. Architecture was reserved for the fortunate few, for military and political leaders and representatives of God on Earth. The artistically beautiful architecture this generated dominated landscape and nature in every respect. Exclusive materials were preferred, craftsmen and artists were brought from near and far, and no expense was spared. Ordinary people in rural communities, however, built completely differently. They built in a manner adapted to the climate, to the materials and resources provided by nature and to the techniques available. That meant building with wood, peat, clay, reeds, turf and stone and making use of the ground. Many people also found accommodation in homes hewn from rock.

Back to nature

In the 18th century, the Age of Enlightenment, a change in the detached relationship with nature also became evident in architecture. The virtues of the common man and the 'noble savage's' harmonious relationship with nature were idealised. In the Romantic Movement, ironically, that glorification led to a wave of primitive constructions for the super-rich. These were not meant for living in, of course, but as follies in the landscaped parks surrounding country estates and pleasure gardens. The cottages and grottoes one sees everywhere, like those in England's Stourhead, are renderings of the dwellings of primitive peoples. Strategically placed at focal points in artificial landscapes, they are eminently suitable as hunting lodges, studios or tea pavilions.

The industrial revolution wrought enormous changes in society. Technological progress confirmed humanity's sense of supremacy. We were the masters not only of nature, but also of the laws of nature. By the 19th century, it seems, the seed was sown for the polarisation characteristic of contemporary society. On the one hand, there is technological euphoria and unbridled materialism, on the other, a movement dedicated to establishing a sustainable society that harmonises the development of prosperity with natural processes. Both trends also appeared in architecture, with the industrial architecture of 20th century modernism setting the tone.

Beginning in the late 19th century, trends emerged that attempted to create associations with nature by using natural forms and motifs drawn from plants, minerals and crystals. The Arts and Crafts movement, Art Nouveau, the *Wiener Secession*, the Amsterdam School and the organic method of building, stemming from the anthroposophy of Rudolf Steiner, are just a few of the successive architectural trends of the past hundred years. Initially, the search for a renewed link with nature was nostalgic. Contemporary sustainable

Church
Lalibella,
Ethiopia

Cloister Sainte-Marie de
la Tourette
Eveux-sur-Arbresle,
France
Le Corbusier

13

architecture, however, is increasingly conditioned by intelligent technologies geared to the processes of nature. This is a constant theme in work by architects such as Foster, Piano and Ambasz.

Misery

The rediscovery of subterranean construction during the industrial revolution was not especially positive. During mass urban migrations, factory workers were housed in cellars and basements, in cold, damp, badly ventilated rooms. The proletariat lived in unhygienic, unhealthy, wretched conditions. At the end of the 19th century, some 20,000 people lived in basements in Amsterdam alone. Aboveground city expansion primarily accommodated the rapidly growing middle class, who wanted, like the old elites, to live well in spacious surroundings. In the Netherlands, this situation came to an end in 1901, when the Housing Act enabled town councils to combat this underground misery.

Le Corbusier

Although modernism can hardly be accused of a strong focus on nature, its links with the landscape and nature are nevertheless clearly visible in a very personal manner in the works of two charismatic representatives of the International Style.

Although nature is a constant and central theme in the work of Le Corbusier, in this he is certainly not rigid. Strongly rational and intellectual at times, at others he was more intuitive and spiritual. His earlier buildings are white, detached and built literally above the ground, set on legs. The ground itself is left virgin and undisturbed,

14 UNDERDEVELOPED

For many film directors, the underworld is a symbol of the incomprehensible, the criminal or the terrifying. But the underground is also the scene of spectacular adventures, as, for example, in the impressively designed gothic caves in Lord of the Rings, where the heroes are besieged by 'evil' in all its forms. James Bond and Indiana Jones are also usually put to the test in breathtaking subterranean settings, from which each always emerges as vanquisher.

In the futuristic masterpiece, Metropolis, from 1926, Fritz Lang proffers a polarised vision of the 21st century city. Workers live and work under ground in degrading conditions. Thanks to their slaves, the city-dwellers above ground lead wonderful, easy lives. In Metropolis, the aboveground ruling class is literally over the workers, who never see a single ray of sunlight.

In THX1138, George Lucas' first film, you don't notice at first that life is going on under ground. The apparent reality is a clinically inhuman world. Only at the end, when the main character emerges into a dazzling sunrise after being pursued through endless tunnels, does it become clear that the entire narrative has transpired below ground. In Matrix, the contrary is true. There, a familiar reality only exists virtually to conceal from people their terrible underground reality, that they are being kept just like a colony of ants keeps aphids.

Cellars and tombs, places from where the living dead operate, seem to appeal to the imaginations that create thrillers and horror stories. Frankenstein – the monster sewn together in a cellar – and Dracula – sleeping during the day in a coffin in a crypt – are well-know examples that have been repeatedly filmed. The underground is also the place for living out sinister (sexual) fantasies. In Pulp Fiction, one of the most oppressive scenes takes place in an subterranean SM den.

There are also people so ugly they would rather not leave their underground refuges, like the creature in Beauty and the Beast, who feels more at home shut away in his secluded underworld than in the outside air. Living beneath the ground enables him to be himself. But life underground is rarely one of choice, for subterranean existence is generally obligatory, as in primitive dungeons and prisons.

while the roof is the place for laying out a garden or terrace. It is almost as though Le Corbusier's buildings are not allowed to touch the ground, as with his Villa Savoye of 1931. But his early work is not aloof. There, architectonic structures were clearly related to their environments, and a building was a place from which to contemplate the surroundings. In his later work, the relationship to nature is radically different, its essence the integration of building into the environment. The relationship with nature becomes tangible, more colourful, earthier. His floating, white 'machines' cede to sturdy monolithic forms, sometimes submerged beneath the soil. Le Corbusier combines natural and geometric forms, as can be seen distinctly in his *pièce de resistance*, the Notre Dame du Haut in Ronchamp, from 1955. Part of the structure lies underground, as the adjacent residences for the clergy are submerged in the hill. The chapel of the Sainte-Marie de la Tourette monastery is also submerged in the earth, its introverted location emphasised by the mystical fall of light from above.

Le Corbusier was already seeking that meditative, introspective quality in his design for an underground basilica dedicated to Mary Magdalene, to be hewn entirely from rock. To Le Corbusier's great regret, the church, to be built in a place of pilgrimage, Sainte-Baume in Provence, was never realised. He commented that it would have been an extraordinary architectonic enterprise, 'an immense, invisible effort to realise the interior, intended to transport only those souls who could comprehend it. It is a building without an exterior, but the architecture would have come to life within the rock.'

Not only cellars, but also metros, sewers, tunnels and car parks are eminently suitable as film sets. Luc Besson's Subway *takes place entirely in the metro, where the characters live. In Le Dernier Metro by Francois Truffaut, the metro primarily represents an opportunity to flee.*

One of the most wonderful examples of an underground film is Orson Welles' The Third Man. *The main character disappears into the sewers of war-torn Vienna, while the city is embroiled in anarchic chaos. Paradoxically, not the underworld is in turmoil, but the visible urban society, In the end, the hero manages to work his way through the endless tunnels. Shot entirely in contrast-rich black and white, the film has fantastic sets, and the extended chase through the sewerage system is especially spectacular. Sophisticated lighting gives the sewers a ghostly glimmer, as repulsive as it is beautiful.*

Frankenstein
Director: James Whale

Lucille Halsell
Conservatory
Texas, USA
Emilio Ambasz

Frank Lloyd Wright

Frank Lloyd Wright's works are not typically modernist. His buildings are not notable for the use of simple volumes, steel, glass and columns, brilliant white, and transparent facades. But the open spaciousness of his designs makes him a modernist nonetheless. Frank Lloyd Wright strives for architecture that develops from the inside outwards, and is in harmony with its exterior. Because his architecture is not rational, but comes from the heart, and because he incorporates time, growth and development into his designs, it is often referred to as organic. Inspired by the traditional architecture of Japan and of the Pueblo Indians, he achieves external harmony by making his buildings part of their surroundings. Their affinity with the landscape only becomes stronger with the passage of time. Taliesin West, Wright's own house and studio in the Arizona desert, appears to grow right out of the ground. It is a symbiosis, Wright's personal, intuitive and, above all, poetic response to the surrounding countryside. Some of Frank Lloyd Wright's houses are literally integrated into the landscape, partly dug in or with embankments built up against them. His Herbert Jacobs house in Wisconsin is embedded into the landscape in this way, its outward form appearing to rise from a hill, the bottom floor submerged. The ground embraces the house, offering protection to the north and opening to the south, where the house faces the sun.

Architecture 'that gives back'

Although these buildings were submerged and covered with earth primarily for purposes of aesthetic expression, they gained a kind of prophetic significance after the alarming reports by the Club of Rome and the energy crisis of the 1970s. In America, the result was the unprecedented popularity of earth-covered residences, also partly due to publications of the Underground Space Center in Minneapolis. The pioneer of the earth-covered renaissance, John Carmody, discusses the subject in an interview in this book. Many of the houses from the underground building boom were characterised by well-intentioned amateurism, inspired by exaggerated yearnings for autarkic buildings. There are, however, some wonderful examples from that time, such as the Forest House and the Dune Houses in Florida, designed by William Morgan. In the latter case, two adjacent egg-shaped structures are incorporated into a dune. Two large openings, the only holes in the dune apart from the entrance, form loggias overlooking the Atlantic Ocean. The Forest House, also in Florida, consists of two pyramids covered with earth, the larger a house,

Project 222
Pembrokeshire, Wales
Great Britain
Future Systems

EFA **Radio Satellite**
Station
Aflenz, Austria
Gustav Peichl

17

the smaller a garage. The pyramids were partially opened to admit light and provide views to the outside. Even Philip Johnson, exponent *pur sang* of modernist construction, has two earth-covered buildings to his name, both designed to leave their beautiful scenic surroundings as intact as possible: The Geier House in Cincinnati, from 1965, and an underground pavilion for his art collection, built on the modern estate of New Canaan in Connecticut. More recent are Jersey Devil's Hill House in California and Project 222 by Future Systems in Wales. Both of these earth-covered villas are sited at spectacular coastal locations. The architects harmonised both houses with their desolate surroundings so that they merge into their environments, while glorious panoramic views can be enjoyed from within.

The essential theme of Emilio Ambasz' work is the relationship with the environment. Since the early 1970s, he has been constructing buildings that seek connections with the earth at every level – aesthetic, ecological, philosophical, poetic. In a discussion I had with him for this book, he spoke of 'architecture that gives back'.

It was less the design principle of 'giving back' than that of maximum integration into the landscape that prompted Gustav Peichl to situate his broadcasting station in Aflenz, Austria, underground. Which seems all the more remarkable as this modern technological facility is aimed at the cosmos itself.

Architecture without Architects

In 1964, Bernard Rudofsky compiled an exhibition that transformed the way architecture was viewed. In *Architecture without Architects*, not architecture with a capital 'A' was placed within the walls of the Museum of Modern Art in New York, but local, indigenous and traditional architecture. This was a revolutionary concept, since the history of architecture had always concentrated on buildings for the established order. Palaces and castles for the nobility, cathedrals and monasteries for the clergy, parliamentary buildings and town halls for the patricians and villas and country houses for the moneyed classes. The exhibition broke with that tradition, but also with the custom of studying only buildings from the West, and primarily from Europe. In a book with the same title, published for the exhibition, there was an old black and white photograph of underground dwellings in China. When I saw the book in the early 1980s, I found it one of the most intriguing pictures, showing a couple of barely visible, inhabited holes in flat terrain. A few years later, I saw the Yao Dongs with my own eyes.

Yao Dong
Near Xian, China

Cave complex
Capadocia, Turkey

The Yao Dong

A Yao Dong is a kind of submerged patio house. The patio, a rectangular hole in the ground, is roughly eight by ten metres and six to seven metres deep. A tree in the sunken courtyard provides shade in the summer. Sometimes, the kitchen, or rather cooking area, is housed in a separate building in the courtyard to keep smoke away from the living quarters. The Yao Dong is perfectly consistent with the Chinese style of living, strongly introvert in character and focussed on the family. Chinese houses are always arranged around a courtyard and are entirely closed off from the outside world, oriented to the safe, enclosed, private domain of the family. The patio is dug out with simple tools. The firm loessial soil ensures that the vertical walls around the patio simply remain standing. Various rooms are then excavated according to requirement: narrow, tunnel-like rooms. The strength of the ground determines how widely and how much can be excavated. Whole villages are dug out in this way in a sort of draughtboard pattern. Excavated earth is used for building other houses at ground level. The thick construction walls are made by manually tamping down the earth in simple forms. The result is a combination of sunken patio houses and simple adobe architecture. And it means, above all, manual work – digging and stamping. But there is usually no shortage of helping hands and feet in China.

People have lived in Yao Dongs since at least 5000 BC. An estimated 40 million Chinese still live underground in the provinces of Shanxi, Shensi, Henan and Kansu. The Yao Dongs' success is explained by the scarcity of building materials and the extreme climate. Space is created by taking something away, and little more need be added than a couple of wooden windows and doors. Due to the virtually constant underground temperature, a Yao Dong is relatively cool in the hot summers and relatively warm in the cold winters. Moreover, a subterranean location offers protection from the hard, cold, sandy winds from Siberia and Mongolia that sweep northern China.

During Mao's rule, this rural way of living was strongly promoted. This may seem odd, since all links with traditional China were severed during the Cultural Revolution, but it fitted in well with the agricultural policy. With scarce fertile land, they could not afford to lose more productive topsoil than necessary. Mao himself also had a lasting personal relationship with the underground. After the Long March, the headquarters of the Communist Party was housed in cave dwellings for more than ten years. After he came to power in Beijing, fear of confrontation with Russia led him to have a complete subterranean city built under Beijing, designed to survive a nuclear holocaust.

Musée des Graffiti
Niaux, France
Massimiliano Fuksas

The cave and the tent

Knowledge of the protection offered by the underground is as old as humanity itself. Human communities have lived and sheltered in natural caves for at least 100,000 years. In my interview with Norman Foster, he names the cave as one of architecture's two archetypes, the other being the tent. All later building forms, he says, are derived from these two. No wonder caves and tents evoke such romantic images for so many people.

In Europe, the caves of Lascaux are, without doubt, the most famous. Whether people lived in them permanently, whether they offered temporary accommodation for nomadic hunters, or whether they were never inhabited at all, but were instead a ritual site, we do not know. We can admire the paintings, but the rest is simply conjecture. We do know, however, that there were a large number of cave dwellings in virtually every Mediterranean country, located not in natural caves like those in Lascaux, but hewn from rock. Nowadays, practically no one lives in rock dwellings, but they were still inhabited until far into the 20th century. In Andalusia, in southern Spain, there are still a number of village communities many of whose houses were cut from living stone.

Although, typologically speaking, there are only actually two forms of underground dwelling, the 'hollow in the rock' and the 'hole in the ground', the variation is nevertheless very wide, depending on landscape, soil type and type of stone. The wealth of different forms has led to some surprising combinations. In Capadocia, in Turkey, for example, whole villages were hewn from a surrealistic landscape of stalactites. The area is situated in the middle of nowhere, ideal for early Christian communities persecuted by the Romans. For more than a thousand years, Christians have cut homes, churches and even complete monasteries from the easily worked tuff rock. Located in the long-deserted towers of an eroded volcanic landscape, the complex underground systems are now major tourist attractions.

Attraction

We love to descend underground on holiday. The caves of Han, in Belgium, attract thousands of vacationers each year, like those in Valkenburg aan de Geul, where a visit to the marl pits and coal mines is a regular part of many school trips. In the past, it was the raw materials mined there that were of essential importance; now it is the space they left behind. To provide a creative function for the caves, an international competition was held to solicit ideas, under the name of Atlantis 2000. The flood of inspiring images and ideas submitted showed that the underground provides designers with a challenge that gives their imaginations full rein.

That same freedom of design can be seen in the expressive entrance Massimiliano Fuksas constructed for the prehistoric Niaux caves. It is often said that, with subterranean building, the entrance is the most important design element. Fuksas made far more than a mere entrance. It is a complete route, which welcomes you with open arms and guides you into the interior of the caves.

In the Spanish city of Toledo, Lapeña & Torres also built a route sunk into the ground. A cleft in the mountainside links the city high up in the mountains with the valley. Tourists can ascend directly from the car park via a cascade of escalators.

The passage through the earth is also an important aspect of the Vulcania underground museum in Saint-Ours les Roches in Auvergne, completed in 2002. A long descent leads visitors, as if through an eroded valley, to a funnel-shaped artificial crater, the heart of the volcano museum. The complex of buildings has strongly symbolic connotations. You do not go there, however, to pray to the forces of nature, but to learn about them. In this museum, designed by Hans Hollein, you can see what happens under the earth – literally. Hollein had prior experience designing an excavated museum. In 1989, he won first prize in a design competition for the Guggenheim Museum in Salzburg. The museum would have had no exterior, but instead an unprecedented sculptural interior, which would have been entirely hewn from the Mönchberg. This literally gave form to the remark by Lao-Tse: 'Architecture is what remains when you remove the walls.' Both museums have unusual plans, which could never have been realised aboveground – nor would anyone have wanted to. They are both octopus-like, moving freely in all directions, probing their tentacles into the most appealing places around them.

20

Spanish stairs
Toledo, Spain
Lapeña & Torres

In touch

Mountains and caves are often especially significant as holy places. In elevated places, you are released from the earthly environment, which allows contact with the celestial. In places deep in the earth, you are in touch with the origins of life, with Mother Earth herself.

Between 300 and 1300 AD, the Anasazi Indians built their pueblos around the Four Corners area (Arizona, Colorado, New Mexico, Utah). The remains are strikingly well preserved. Indian tradition is marked by a deep-rooted respect for ancestors and avoids disturbing their former dwelling places. In the famous pueblos of Chaco Canyon and Mesa Verde, there are a remarkable number of round holes made in the ground, the kivas, or religious chambers of the Anasazi symbolising the Earth Mother. Initially, the Anasazi also lived in round holes in the ground, but after the pueblos were built, they started living aboveground. The ritual chambers, however, remained under ground. Modern day Pueblo Indians, such as the Hopi, still use subterranean kivas for religious ceremonies.

In India, enormous temple complexes have been cut from solid rock. The space 'freed' from the solid mass has deep spiritual significance in both Buddhism and Hinduism. In a place made in this way, monks can bring themselves into harmony with the life-creating energy and essence of the earth itself. A room excavated from the earth also has a sexual connotation: penetration into the womb of the earth, from which all life springs.

In the 13th century, near Lalibella in Ethiopia, Christians created the famous churches hewn from rock. Only the roofs are noticeable, for the rest of the buildings are underground. The churches and the spaces around them are entirely hewn from the living rock of the substratum. Once the exterior was formed, a mono-lithic church was hollowed out to form an interior.

Throughout history, sacred chambers have been made in and under the ground, even by modern architects. This book contains other examples in addition to the aforementioned holy places. Suomalainen's Temppeliaukio Church, Yamaguchi's Glass Temple and Niemeyer's Catedral Metropolitana all use underground spaces to drama-tise architecturally the contrast between worldly and divine dimensions. Tadao Ando should also be mentioned in this context. His integration of architecture and landscape is strongly reminiscent of the traditional Japanese Zen garden. While all his works exude a calm, meditative ambience, his Water Temple in Hyogo is the epitome

Vulcania Museum
Saint-Ours les Roches,
France
Hans Hollein

Augusteum Guggenheim Museum
Salzburg, Austria
Hans Hollein

Water Temple
Tsuna-gun, Hyogo, Japan
Tadao Ando

of eloquent simplicity. In the Buddhist story of creation, water was the first element to come into the world. From water was born the lotus, symbol of the Buddha's spiritual awakening. The roof of the oval temple is a lotus pool. By means of a narrow staircase cut into the pool, the visitor descends to the serene temple underground. The path taken by the visitor through the water frees him from daily preoccupations and prepares him for the transcendental.

Not to be

It is natural to find peace in an underground room. The inward, enclosed quality invites you to retreat inside yourself. In our restless society, it is perhaps only there that one can find real tranquillity. The quest for peace is a luxury we allow ourselves only in life's later years. That we find opportunities for meditation, introspection, reflection and rest in underground crypts and temples is not really surprising. That is, after all, where we place our loved ones for their final rest. Depending upon the culture and religion, this is done sometimes quite modestly and sometimes in an extraordinarily lavish fashion.

The monumental tombs in Petra in Jordan, roughly 2000 years old, are world-famous. People often mistake them for rock-hewn churches, but nothing could be further from the truth, for they are actually the burial places of the elite. Egyptian, Greek and Persian influences can be seen in the richly ornamented, sculpted facades. Burial culture in the Netherlands, on the other hand, is very simple. Given the national character, that is not surprising, and it seems things have never been any different. The earth-covered megalithic tombs in the north are remarkable for their simplicity, although their construction, some 5,000 years ago, must have required monumental effort. The Egyptians approached things quite differently: on a grand scale and with great artistry – at least for the pharaohs. Initially they were buried in Pyramids and later, from 1500 BC onward, in tombs cut from the rock. In the Valley of the Kings in Thebes, where the tomb of Tutankhamun was discovered, more than 60 temples to the dead were hollowed out.

The incomparable monumental tombs of the pharaohs lie within the twilight zone between architecture and art. Architecture is born from the marriage of art and science; it is both art and artifice. Unfortunately, underground building all too often leans towards artifice, towards technology. Art, on the other hand, is sadly neglected. Landscape art is the art form that inspires me the most. This trend is not fastidiously conceptual, but translates concepts in an earthy and tangible manner. Such works of art evoke a different conception of the earth and of nature. They invite affinity and inspire the artist to work with what is given. Moreover, the senses are stimulated by images of unprecedented beauty. The works of Robert Smithson and Andy Goldsworthy leave impressions in the earth I would love to measure up to. A dynamic balance is created between presence and restraint, between creating shapes and leaving forms untouched, between what has been made by man and what has always existed.

Church
Lalibella,
Ethiopia

Snow sculpture
Polar circle
Andy Goldsworthy

FRIEDRICHSTRASSE

Berlin

Jean Nouvel, Henri Cobb, Oswald Mathias Ungers

After the fall of the Berlin Wall, the municipality of Berlin wanted to breathe new life into Friedrichstrasse, formerly a fashionable shopping area. This desire was interpreted in three totally different ways by three designers. The Friedrichstadt Passage consists of a series of independent mega structures lining Friedrichstrasse, each of which is multifunctional. Included are offices, residences, shops and parking facilities. What passers-by on street level could never guess is that, in addition to seven storeys aboveground, each unit contains four sublevels. All three units are connected underground by spacious shopping streets.

In an attempt to reintroduce the typical Berlin building style, many of the units along Friedrichstrasse and in the surrounding area have courtyards. Originally intended as semi-public areas, as places for meeting, the courtyards of the new units have been privatised and are no longer publicly accessible. Strictly speaking, the underground passage is not a public area, either. Ironically, despite the success of the hidden passage, it obscures the identity of the public street for visitors, even though it was the original goal of the project to strengten that identity.

No. 207: Jean Nouvel

On the corner of Französische Strasse stands a most remarkable unit: the Galéries Lafayette, designed by the French architect, Jean Nouvel. The four sides and roof of the building are of glass and round at one corner. The innumerable reflections this creates provide a spectacular image. The transparency of the building is enhanced by reflections of artificial light. The masterstroke of the unit is the way the building has been cored. Two cones of glass, placed one on top of the other, bore like a whirlwind through the unit from top to bottom. The first cone reaches its largest diameter at the level of the ground floor and the second tapers downward from that point. The logical result is that natural light penetration is optimised and transported deep down into the building. At ground level, the cone is open, offering a view of all eleven storeys.

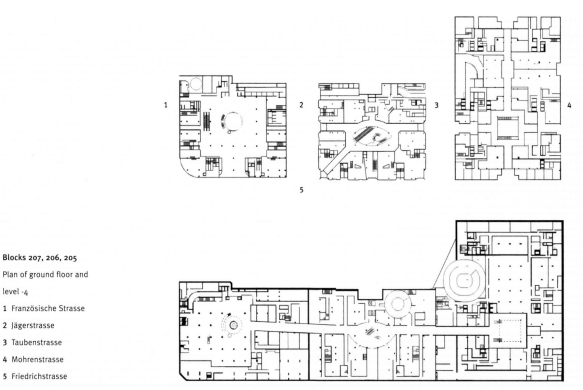

Blocks 207, 206, 205

Plan of ground floor and level -4

1 Französische Strasse

2 Jägerstrasse

3 Taubenstrasse

4 Mohrenstrasse

5 Friedrichstrasse

FRIEDRICHSTRASSE

Function **shopping arcades, offices, homes, parking facilities**

Address **Friedrichstrasse unit No. 207, Berlin, Germany**

Floor surface **40,000 m²**

Depth **12 metres**

Number of levels underground **4**

Construction time **3.5 years**

Initiative **1991**

Design **1991-1993**

Construction **1993-1996**

Client **Dresdner Bank, Roland Ernst, SGE Société Générale d`Entreprise, CBC Compagnie Générale de Bâtiment et de Construction**

Architect **Jean Nouvel, Paris**

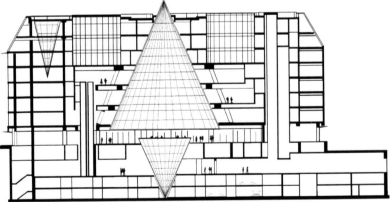

Block 207

Section

Block 207

Interior

No. 206: Henry Cobb

With its fragmented exterior and decorative interior, the centre unit, designed by the American Henry Cobb, harks back to the art deco style of the 1920s. Due to the continuity created by protruding and recessed facade elements, this block, unlike the Nouvel unit, is more contextual. The play of patterns and geometry in the facade is continued in a lens-shaped courtyard, filled with a star-shaped skylight, providing two of the four underground levels with daylight.

Blocks 207 and 206
Street view

Block 206
Interior

30

FRIEDRICHSTRASSE

Function **shopping arcades, offices, homes, parking facilities**

Address **Friedrichstrasse unit No. 206, Berlin, Germany**

Floor surface **44,500 m²**

Depth **12 metres**

Number of levels underground **4**

Construction time **3.5 years**

Initiative **1991**

Design **1991-1993**

Construction **1993-1996**

Client **Jagdfeld Friedrichstadtpassagen**

Architect **Henry Cobb, New York**

No. 205: Oswald Mathias Ungers

The building units all respect the 22-metre gutter height and the building line of the neighbouring units. Unit 205, designed by German architect Oswald Mathias Ungers, readily joins the line. Ungers' right-angled form language, however, pales somewhat in comparison with the curves of Nouvel and Cobb's crystalline forms. The solid, eight-storey building is marked by the protruding volume of the first five storeys, with the recessed entrances to the shops. The facade forms a restful background for historic buildings around the Platz der Akademie. Underground, the visitor's attention is continually drawn by the high-quality range of shops, leaving no time or space for prejudices against being underground. Nor is there any reason for such prejudices in Ungers' functional environment; the areas are light and spacious.

FRIEDRICHSTRASSE

Function **shopping arcades, offices, homes, parking facilities**

Address **Friedrichstrasse unit No. 205, Berlin, Germany**

Floor surface **52,000 m²**

Depth **12 metres**

Number of levels underground **4**

Construction time **3.5 years**

Initiative **1991**

Design **1991-1993**

Construction **1993-1996**

Client **Tishman Speyer Properties Deutschland Gmbh**

Architect **Oswald Mathias Ungers, Cologne**

HOLMES PLACE
Coming Soon, 1. Oktober 2001
Männersache
AVEDA
EG Passage
Foodcourt
Quartier 205

MUSEUMPLEIN
Amsterdam

Kees Spanjer, Kisho Kurokawa et al.

MUSEUMPLEIN, ALBERT HEIJN

Function **supermarket**

Address **Van Baerlestraat 33b,**

Amsterdam, the Netherlands

Construction volume **8,000 m³**

Floor surface **2,000 m²**

Depth **4 metres**

Number of levels underground **1**

Construction time **3 years**

Initiative **1990**

Design **1993-1995**

Construction **1997-1999**

Client **ING Vastgoed BV**

Architects **Zaanen Spanjers CS**

Architects, Amsterdam

Engineers **Arcadis Bouw/Infra,**

The Hague

The 'Ezelsoor'

Car park entrance

In order to preserve historic inner cities such as Amsterdam's, underground building seems the only viable strategy. In 1990, when the reorganisation of Museumplein was planned, a second level below ground seemed the most appropriate solution for the coming 21st century. Architect and artist John Körmeling proposed paving the entire breadth of Museumplein, creating the widest and shortest motorway in the Netherlands. You could say that Danish designer Sven-Ingvar Andersson executed Körmeling's plan – if now transformed spatially. He replaced the asphalt with a friendlier surface – a large uninterrupted plain of grass running from the Rijksmuseum to the Concertgebouw – and instead of allowing vehicles on it, submerged them under it. The plan has proved a great success for both visitors to the area and those just passing through.

In addition to a car park for passenger cars, the Museumplein underground programme consists of a coach park, a supermarket, an extension to the Van Gogh Museum, the goods supply to the Rijksmuseum and the loveliest public lavatories in Amsterdam. The space under ground level, designed with such care and attentiveness, makes Museumplein more than simply a green carpet beneath which certain necessary but preferably unseen functions are swept away.

Car parks

Parking problems in the vicinity of Museumplein prompted the construction of two underground car parks. Congestion was caused not only by passenger cars, but primarily by large numbers of coaches. Architect Kees Spanjer designed a chic coach terminal, its entrance on Paulus Potterstraat and its exit on Hobbemastraat to ensure a smooth flow of traffic. The coach terminal, which can be used in the evenings for passenger vehicles, is linked underground to the Rijksmuseum for loading and unloading goods at the watertight subterranean storage depots. Pedestrian entrances to the underworld are located in two beautifully designed pavilions, which also house the museum shop, the Cobra Café and public lavatories.

The two-storey car park for passenger cars is on the south side of the square, on Van Baerlestraat, and accommodates six hundred cars. Pedestrian entrances take the form of luxurious glass pavilions located on the square. A light strip, running the length of the ceiling and over Museumplein, provides natural lighting of the convenient passageway that leads pedestrians to levels -1 and -2. The profusion of light on the pastel-coloured walls and the organised layout generate a great feeling of security. No wonder it was proclaimed the best European car park of 2001.

Both car parks have been fitted with an impulse ventilator system; based on longitudinal ventilation, the air is kept constantly moving. Fresh air enters via the entrances and exits and is extracted via shafts. It is driven by sensors, enabling the system to respond efficiently in the event of fire or smoke. Smoke development is limited by the layout of the compartments, and any smoke can be extracted locally at high speed, via shafts.

Construction of the car park followed the polder principle, consisting of twenty-metre deep sheetpile walls topped with concrete beams. When the polder floor was laid, however, a water-repellent layer at a depth of thirteen metres proved not to be entirely watertight. It turned out that the soil survey had not been thorough enough to discover holes. A concrete floor with tension piles was then added.

MUSEUMPLEIN, CAR PARKS

Function **car park**

Address **Van Baerlestraat 33b,**

Amsterdam, the Netherlands

Construction volume **119,000 m³**

Floor surface **21,000 m²**

Depth **7 metres**

Number of levels underground **2**

Construction time **3 years**

Initiative **1990**

Design **1993-1995**

Construction **1995-1997**

Client **ING Vastgoed BV in collaboration**

with Stadsdeel Zuid

Architects **Zaanen Spanjers cs Architects,**

Amsterdam

Supermarket

Initially, the Albert Heijn supermarket chain was very hesitant about underground construction. The need for customers to travel vertically was seen as an obstacle. Given the absence of a physically visible building, the shop needed to profile itself in some other way. The *'Ezelsoor,'* or 'Dog-Ear,' a corner of the Museumplein that is folded upwards, was the deciding factor. Customers can enter the shop through a more-or-less normal entrance, which provides an identifiable landmark. A second access from the car park removes every obstacle for customers, who can load shopping into their cars at the same level. Visitors will barely realise that no daylight penetrates underground. After all, consumers have been shopping for years in introverted shopping centres. And with good reason: research shows that daylight and outside views influence purchasing behaviour negatively.

Van Gogh Museum Extension

On the west side of Museumplein stands a solid, enclosed block, designed by Japanese architect Kisho Kurokawa. His preference for geometric forms can be seen in the oval-shaped extension. The oval is divided into two, and the aboveground half, which borders the square, houses new exhibition rooms. The other half forms a submerged patio with a shallow pond below. Leaning over the balustrade of this lion's den, the height, or rather the depth, of this building becomes clear. The extension consists of three storeys with a total of 2,250 m^2 of exhibition surface, two-thirds of it below ground level. The new wing is accessible only from the entrance of Rietveld's cubist main building. The transitional area leading from the angular building to the curved one, lying within Rietveld's building, was designed by Martien van Goor of Greiner Van Goor Architects BV. Here, visitors descend seven and a half metres by escalator to the patio level. *De Knoop*, or The Knot, as the zone is called, flows over into a promenade that surrounds a pond, a still courtyard that, while devoid of any form of vegetation, is still reminiscent of a Japanese garden. With a million visitors annually, the extension provides the Van Gogh Museum with essential air and space.

40

Museumplein

1 Pedestrian entrance to coach park

2 Coach park entrance

3 Coach park exit

4 To the Rijksmuseum

5 Van Gogh Museum

6 Van Gogh Museum extension

7 Stedelijk Museum

8 Supermarket

9 Concertgebouw

10 Pedestrian entrance to car park

11 Car park entrance

12 Car park exit

13 Van Baerlestraat

14 Paulus Potterstraat

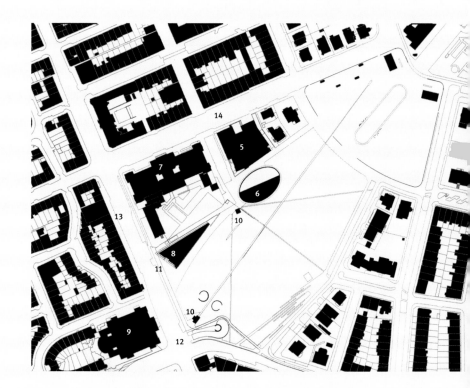

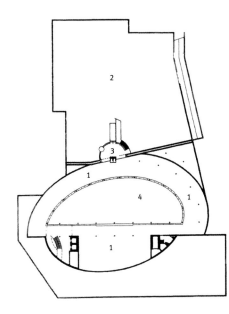

MUSEUMPLEIN, VAN GOGH MUSEUM

Function **museum**

Address **Paulus Potterstraat 7, Amsterdam, the Netherlands**

Construction volume **20,000 m³**

Floor surface **5,000 m²**

Depth **7.5 metres**

Number of levels underground **1**

Initiative **1990**

Design **1990**

Construction **up to 1998**

Client **Van Gogh Museum**

Architects **Kisho Kurokawa, Greiner Van Goor Architects BV, Amsterdam**

Engineers **F.B. Architectural Agency of Rotterdam**

Van Gogh Museum

Patio

Van Gogh Museum
Cross-section and
longitudinal section

Van Gogh Museum
'de Knoop'

First green, then grey, then green again

Interview with Emilio Ambasz

Since its establishment in New York, the architects' firm of Emilio Ambasz has demonstrated that neither small-scale nor large-scale projects have to be realised according to the rules of conventional architecture. To enable a building to exist in optimal harmony with its environment, Ambasz prefers promoting a green variety of architecture, covering grey concrete with green trees, grass and bushes, allowing a building's roof to fulfil the function of a park, garden or landscape. His Green over Grey results in architecture that 'gives back' to society, which is especially desirable in countries with high land prices.

Literally speaking, the lion's share of Emilio Ambasz' buildings can be termed underground architecture. However, he seldom seeks solutions literally under ground level. As a rule, he creates an artificial hill partly covering facades, and often the entire roof, with earth. Still, the Casa de Retiro Espiritual, built by Ambasz more than 25 years ago in Cordoba, is a 'real' underground construction. Ambasz: 'For me, it demonstrates that you don't need to produce architecture according to a canon. You can invoke the presence and essence of architecture without elements such as windows or columns.' Inspired by a traditional Andalusian concept, this weekend house has a central submerged patio, onto which all the rooms open. 'The house is extremely light, because I used a lot of glass. The light is reflected by two large, white, stuccoed walls, which protrude above ground. Although the rooms are always in shadow, as the house has a northern aspect, the strong reflections compensate for this. That's very important to me. A house has to function, every little part of it. Everything is pragmatic, functional.' The Casa de Retiro Espiritual blends so well into its surroundings that it is as if the building has always been there.

Casa de Retiro Espiritual
Cordoba, Spain

'Other buildings stand there as if they're on pieces of woodland cleared by burning. The house is even more attractive if you see it in real life. It might sound a bit over the top, but it has really touched some people's hearts. They think it's great.'

Architecture 'giving back'

Ambasz' unconventional Green over Grey method offers a solution in cities where the last open green spaces are threatening to disappear. From the beginning of his career, the Argentinean architect set himself the task of realising projects that give space back. His buildings are often wholly or partially covered by parks and gardens with free access to the public. This is his way of returning space to society, and it also generates extraordinary experiences, says Ambasz: 'When you visit one of my buildings, you experience it in the same way as any other building. You don't realise there are worms above your head. But when you go outside and turn around, you don't see the building any more.' The government building in Fukuoka, Japan, is a classic example. The construction of the complex office building was to have meant sacrificing the last park in the city centre, which created a lot of resistance. But Ambasz suggested to the planning commission that the park could be reconstructed in terrace form, and distributed over the fourteen-storey building. Visitors to the park would be able to walk up from the ground or, without it disturbing the effect, take the lift to a roof garden. Ambasz wanted direct contact with the ground. His successful reconciliation of two opposing claims to space at the same location generated a lot of support amongst the local population.

Not only in cities, but in rural areas as well, Ambasz prefers architecture that gives something back: 'What I try to do is keep land intended for agricultural use as agricultural land. But with a building as well, so you have both. Naturally, not all buildings are suitable, but it does work in some cases.' One example is the Dutch town of Hilversum, where Ambasz was responsible for designing a sizeable office complex adjacent to a nature reserve. Not one millimetre of green was sacrificed, for all three office blocks are incorporated into a terrace-like, artificial hill.

Artificial nature

Ambasz' designs, he believes, show that architecture is an integral part of the cultural landscape. 'You have to realise that in Europe and, for example, Japan, too, an artificial form of nature has been created, 'the garden", he explains. 'The garden emerged when men were still building temples on hills to invoke the gods. In this context, the idea emerged that man was master of nature. We started designing nature and made a different kind,

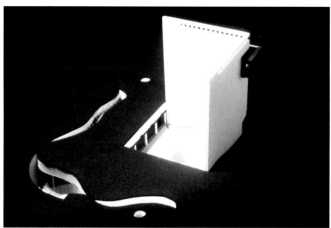

an artificial nature. We have never really perceived architecture as part of that artificial nature. Of course, once you have artificial nature, that prompts the philosophical question of what we understand by the term 'nature'. What we need is a philosophical definition of the word. Nature has always been society's hope and concern. That's way above the poor architect's head. So what I attempt to do is treat architecture as the origin of artificial nature, which is why I create artificial, surrealistic landscapes, which I call realistic. That's why the models I make are so different in respect of architectonic tradition. Models can be very realistic, with trees made of wood and green grass. If you look at my buildings and houses in Montana, Andalusia and Japan and the botanical garden in Texas, you will see that the landscape has turned out more or less as the model showed. The running gag in my office is that, when my assistant sees photographs of my buildings, she always says, 'They look just like your models.'

The integration of artificial nature and architecture is a leitmotiv in Ambasz' work. He takes such integration even further and calls his methodology, at the risk of sounding 'New Age,' the design tradition of the whole. According to Ambasz, this means opposing the accepted practice of separating living, work and recreation from one another, as is also the case in the Netherlands. 'The green ecological corridors are no more than small, narrow areas of a few kilometres, where people can walk blindfolded. They fulfil a certain purpose, but I don't think it's the solution. It's a partial solution, but you have to think on a larger scale. I could never live without green.'

When towns began to form, says Ambasz, architecture and artificial nature became separated from each other. That can be seen, for example, in the garden cities. 'The centre is the city, around which the garden has been layed out,' he explains. 'In this system, the two are separated: work in the centre and home on the outskirts. Then came modernism. They promised us a house in the garden. The house took up 40 percent of the land,

46

Office complex

Hilversum,

the Netherlands

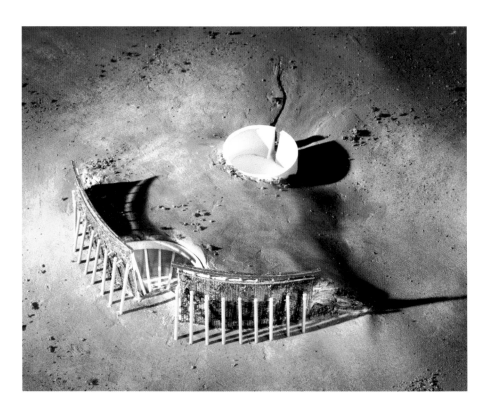

leaving 60 percent garden. That's better, but it's not enough. You see, I don't believe you can make a separation between such emotionally different worlds, with the city on one side and the garden on the other. We want 100 percent garden and 100 percent house.'

Planning permission

Ambasz has noticed that the current generation of civil servants often responds sympathetically to his design proposals. The Japanese government, for example, was so pleased with his design for the Mycal Sanda that they gave the client a 60 percent discount on the land. And that is quite something for Japan, since, as Ambasz says, 'make no mistake, in Tokyo, for example, the ground is fifteen times as expensive as the building.' Something similar also happened in Fukuoka. 'My client offered seven million dollars annual rent for the plot', he explains. 'Normally, he would lose out to someone offering twenty million, which is what the city wanted. Ultimately, the perfect integration of my project into the environment was the decisive factor. This made it a great commercial success for my client.'

Project developers like working with Ambasz, not only because investments in his buildings earn returns. Experience shows that his designs are quickly approved by the authorities. He was once visited by an Italian project developer. 'I explained my way of working to him and calculated that the fee would come to x amount. He said, 'I'll pay you x plus twenty percent'. That meant he needed me immediately to realise that project. He was prepared to pay more because my design guaranteed approval from the authorities.'

But Ambasz has little sympathy for project developers. 'Developers are primarily interested in profit. I, on the other hand, am aware that architecture first and foremost costs money. I once did a little survey and discovered

Prefectural International Hall

Fukuoka, Japan

that architecture in an emphatic sense has a chance only when interest rates are lower than 5 percent annually. If rates are higher, then the extra investment is too great. And good architecture is even more expensive. Not every project developer is willing to take that on. So I have to think of something with which developers can make their money back. Rapid procedures for example, or extra programmes.' At Nuova Concordia, a large-scale housing project on the Ionic Sea in the southernmost part of Italy, Ambasz put that idea into practice. 'The client had waited fourteen years for a building permit and when they found out that the people there didn't want any tower blocks, they looked me up. Two months later, I had the models made and a month later, we got permission to build.' Instead of a complex of high rise apartment blocks, Ambasz had proposed accommodating low residential buildings and villas, together with public and commercial structures such as a hotel, sports facilities, a shopping centre and a conference centre, in an integral, undulating, green, landscaped concept. He converted an intensively built-up district into a park-like environment for everyone to use, leaving the scenic value of the area as intact as possible.

Like a lonely monk

Because he constantly wrestles with producing designs that enrich the environment, Ambasz prefers to see himself as an inventor rather than an architect: 'I have never really seen myself as a professional architect. I only did one year at university, so I had no time to learn anything. I believe the architect must acknowledge an ethical obligation to propose alternative ideas and devise images for what is to come. Images for the future, for a better future. Otherwise, he runs the risk of misusing the present.'

Nouva Concordia Resort
Castellaneta, Italy

Ambasz compares his more conventional colleagues with introverted monks. 'I think it's great that you have monks walking around a monastery discussing how many angels you can fit onto the head of a pin, but the fire is outside. I'm from the same monastery, but I'm walking on the edge of the roof, outside. Like a lonely monk.' Ambasz feels he is part of a new type of architecture. 'All the same, I'm still a child of my time. I'm not the first of my kind. But what I'm doing is still primitive. I'm like a dog trying to run away, although I'm aware of the fact that I still have a chain around my neck. That chain represents the old way of thinking. I'm stuck with my own ideas, with a certain kind of rhetoric. In the future, there will be room for more poetry and talent. I mean a kind of rhetoric involving directly approachable images, which warm the heart. That requires a new way of designing, not an empirical way, or a normative way, but an intuitive way, which we have to learn to understand. We still don't speak that language fluently enough. That certainly goes for the methodologists. I'm intuitive, I design quickly. If a project takes too long, it will never work. I try to find efficient, simple and powerful solutions to show that another kind of architecture is possible.' Here, the green spaces on the roofs of his buildings play a major role. 'These spaces can be either cultivated or neglected. It's everyone's responsibility.'

Schlumberger
Austin, Texas, USA

2 URBAN DEVELOPMENT

The way down is the way out Jaap Huisman

3 km³ Models Amsterdam

Jubilee Line London

THE WAY DOWN IS THE WAY OUT

Using subterranean space on an urban

development scale

Jaap Huisman

In the Netherlands, limited space, soft building ground, the country's historical heritage and increasing concerns about the environment are all leading, without a shadow of a doubt, to a downward orientation. The emergence of the 3D City, one extending both above and below us, with addresses at different heights and depths, seems inevitable. In such an environment, the 'ground' level will disperse into various different levels at once, the square will be replaced by a void, the street by lifts, ramps and escalators. The development of the underground – and therefore the birth of the 3D City – will, however, only succeed if the way is paved psychologically. Users will have to learn to perceive subterranean space as being of equal value to that above ground level.

It is strange how the underworld has managed to retain its magic, while the substratum has been ploughed up and burrowed into by tunnels and metro systems throughout the past century. Its appeal is sometimes based on simple observations, such as the buses in Amsterdam's Paulus Potterstraat, which plunge into a rather narrow channel, disappearing without a trace beneath Museumplein. How fascinating to think of there being thirty or so coaches there at that moment, the same ones that, not so long ago, ruined the view of the of the Rijksmuseum with their gaudy colours. What a relief – good riddance. That fascination comes mainly from the knowledge that they are there, while out of sight. But the whole idea has started us wondering: what else can we shift to the underground level in order to maintain quality of life in the city?

Emancipation of the underworld

As Orpheus discovered when he went in search of his beloved Eurydice, the underworld beckons enticingly. Charon the ferryman rowed him across the river Styx, the border between earth and heaven, life and death,

on a journey to the end of the night. Down below, the twilight is different from the predawn half-light above ground, for it cannot be penetrated at a single glance. Visibility is limited. The best way to experience it is to visit metro stations, only to be surprised again and again at what you find. Sometimes, a station is a cathedral-like vault, like the Moscow metro, but more often a grimy tube, stinking of urine. At one station, a direct route leads to the platform. At another, a lift the size of a removal van transports you what seems like a hundred metres into the bowels of the earth. Then the endless escalators, not to mention the unbelievable distances passengers have to travel before reaching their trains. This is the deceptive effect of the Châtelet/Les Halles station in Paris, or of London's Liverpool Street Station: just when you think you have achieved your objective quickly and easily by popping into the nearest tube station, it turns out to be a Pyrrhic victory. You would have been better off covering the distance above ground, breathing fresh air with the sun on your face. The directionless infinity of underground space is both attractive and repellent. After all, there is no horizon to get your bearings by, only prespectiveless depth.

That underground detour is an unforeseeable disappointment. But there are wonderful experiences to be had, the discoveries under ground level, where buildings bare themselves in their deepest being: their foundations. Whether modern flats or old cloisters, it makes no difference: they all display their strengths underground – otherwise they would never have existed in the first place. Certainly not in the marshy soil of the Netherlands, where pile driving is a *conditio sine qua non.* Putting it irreverently, you could say it is crawl space with columns in between, were it not for the increasing significance of such spaces in the final decades of the 20th century. This is the place where architecture has sought refuge, as there was simply no more room aboveground. In a short period of time, therefore, a system of passages, warehouses, workshops, auditoria and archives has grown, which can be characterised as a *cadavre exquis,* or the merging of archaeology and futurism. On the one hand, we literally see the roots of the existing buildings under which these utility rooms have been built; on the other, we are witness to a new order, one which fires the imagination.

Underground monuments

Increasing concern for the historic heritage of the inner cities is one reason why underground space simply has to be exploited. But not the only one. Traffic congestion and lack of space leave us no way out but downwards.

Museumplein
Amsterdam,
the Netherlands
Sven-Ingvar Andersson

53

Rijksmuseum
Amsterdam,
the Netherlands
Cruz & Ortiz

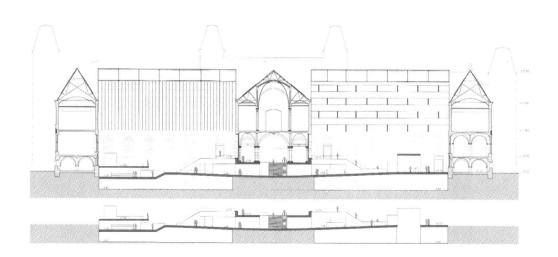

Rijksmuseum
Amsterdam,
the Netherlands
Cruz & Ortiz

Over the past fifteen years, a new stratum has gradually been penetrated. In many cases, this has meant more than just a one-dimensional descent below the surface, the simple addition of basements or cellars to existing buildings. The extensions to the Friesian Museum in Leeuwarden and the Central Museum of Utrecht, for example, are much more than simply basements. They illustrate the new interpretations of subterranean expansion, since, in both cases, they modify historic complexes in centuries-old urban contexts. In Leeuwarden, the picturesque street wall of the Turfmarkt had to remain intact; in Utrecht, the primary objective was the retention of the mediaeval garden behind the Nicolaaskapel. Architect Gunnar Daan connected the existing Friesian Museum to the new wing, located in the monumental Chancellery, via an underground passageway. But that wasn't all. The elliptical tunnel also houses functional rooms, such as the cloakroom and display cases for objects sensitive to direct daylight. In Utrecht, especially, the underground linkages introduced by Flemish architects Beel and Achtergael contribute to the improved organisation of the Central Museum. After renovations, the complex can be seen as a collection of pavilions lying both below and above ground level.

The similarity between the museums in Leeuwarden and Utrecht is that they form bridges between architecture and urban development. In fact, a kind of miniature city has been erected inside each one, extending across several levels and varying in ambience and light. You might conclude that, stimulated by an urban developmental necessity, a natural association has been created between aboveground and underground architecture.

Door to the future

The idea of descending into a museum is nothing less than revolutionary. The classical museum, founded in the 19th century, prepared its visitors for ascent into an artistic Olympus. That was Cuypers' intention when designing the most traditional museum in the Netherlands, the Rijksmuseum. By climbing seemingly endless stairs, the visitor gradually makes his acquaintance with the Arts, with a capital 'A', in the plural form. However colossal it may be, however, the Rijksmuseum is not geared to contemporary logistical requirements or to a demanding public that is looking for more facilities. In renovating the Rijksmuseum, as I.M. Pei did with the Louvre in Paris and the East Wing of the National Gallery in Washington, Spanish architects Cruz and Ortiz opted for a descent, by adding a level under the corridor and the inner courtyards. This can only be seen as a break with 19th century

Mariënburg
Nijmegen,
the Netherlands
Sjoerd Soeters

tradition. At the same time, however, it opens the door to the future. The future of a museum that is aware of its traditions, but also requires transparency and accessibility. Incidentally, Cruz and Ortiz' design is not purely an architectonic panacea. It also acknowledges the double-sidedness of the Rijksmuseum in Amsterdam's planning. After more than a century, the Rijksmuseum now faces both north and south, so the obvious solution is to place the entrance at its heart.

Ramps and escalators

For museums located in historic inner cities, the way down is usually the only possible one for expansion, while in modern or reconstructed centres, such as those in Rotterdam and Nijmegen, the shopping centre has proved to be a tool for revitalising the city. Almost automatically, ground level glides down to level –1, via ramps or escalators, and we enter a 'sheltered', even intimate world, which contrasts with the open structured city above. In both Nijmegen (in Marikenstraat, designed by the architecture firm Soeters Van Eldonk Ponec) and Rotterdam (in Beurstraverse, built to designs by de Architecten Cie/Jon Jerde), differentiated shopping centres were constructed where the public is barely aware what level they are shopping on. How different from old shopping centres where designers had problems palming off basements on retailers, which thus became desolate last resorts for winos and litter. Not exactly an advertisement for underground space.

But urban developers and municipalities have learned from such negative examples. The emphasis has shifted to the organisation and opening up of shopping centres and underground passages. The blind angles and dark recesses that made the Hoog Catharijne centre in Utrecht, for example, intolerable, have been scrapped as far as possible.

Three dimensional inner city

Opening up the underground seems essential to the survival of the historic inner city. In the early 1990s, the municipality of Den Bosch decided to tear up its lovely, if cramped, centre to alleviate pedestrian congestion in the old narrow streets around the market. Monotonous, modernistic blocks of flats behind the north wall of the market made way for an architecture, 'imported' from Spain, which showed more respect for history. The architects/urban developers Joan Busquets and Beth Galí added an anecdotal city quarter to the old centre of Den Bosch, embodied in complexes such as the Stoa and the Arena, the latter of which actually involves the underground. As in Rotterdam and Nijmegen, the transition is painless and smooth. The 'bowl' of the Arena, covered by a floating, square, glass roof, gives the city-dweller the feeling of being in a secluded, Mediterranean square. At least, that is the atmosphere evoked by the terracotta-coloured tiles and plants. Of course, the historic Dutch city owes its success to intimacy and diversity, but an exotic element is clearly no impediment here.

Even a historic inner city that has inflicted the status of a protected cityscape on itself, such as Amsterdam within the Singel canal ring, will not escape subtle expansion. Public space has been pegged out and protected by regulations. Studies by the Rotterdam firm of MVRDV foresee the possibilities that lie underneath the Dam, especially if North-South underground trains are racing past there in a few years time.

Currently, the North-South line is primarily a traffic project, a mobility machine. Little use is being made of the new line, running through the inner city, for the development of new urban areas. In fact, the line is an introverted, autonomous project. Its cohesion with the city is minimal. Elsewhere in the world, however, the construction of a metro line can be a major spur to underground building projects. In Montreal, an almost unprecedented subterranean city has been created between two metro lines. In an interval of thirty-five years, an underground network has been constructed, with stations, shops, car parks and offices. More than a third of all shops in the inner city are located here. In Amsterdam, the network remains – for the present – limited to a combination of metro station and car park.

MVRDV's design study exhaustively explores Amsterdam's underground potential. In accordance with three spatial concepts, the real heart of Amsterdam is 'laid bare'. However futuristic such visions of the monumental

IMPRESSIVE

Komsomolskaya
metro station
Moscow, Russia

'Whenever I go down to take the metro, it's as if time stands still. Here, you could imagine being back in 1960 or 1980', says Svetlana Tretyakova, a retired person. Without exception, Moscow's metro stations are not only ingenious constructions, but also fine examples of palace architecture.

The first metro line dates from the early 1930s. Driven by belief or fear, obedient workers followed Stalin's orders to realise, at any price, the most imposing paragon of the proletarian paradise. Tributes are carved in sculpture and engraved onto plaques, and wall paintings and mosaics bear witness to the achievements of the communist ideal. The lavish architecture, with series of enormous, gilded chandeliers and flamboyant columns resting on polished marble floors, stirs up euphoria even further. Here is a unique collection of stones that would be the envy of many a geological museum. During World War II, the construction of the metro continued tirelessly, combined with the building of air-raid shelters and escape routes. This investment in numerous underground palaces of the people, with their durable materials and spacious systems of passageways, was visionary. Even today, the network, now measuring 200 kilometres, can handle

city may be, the first steps towards the 3D City have already been taken – logically, in a country where scarce space is being fought over. Furthermore, the view that the underground is not a B-location is gaining ground. On the contrary, shopping centres at metro stations, libraries, and underground museums (such as those in Tadao Ando in Japan) all prove that a number of functions can manage perfectly well without daylight.

Underground forces

Still, the geophysics of the *Randstad,* the urban agglomeration of West Holland, will have to cooperate. Up to now, the settling of the ground has been one of the flies in the ointment of underground building, as engineers realised when constructing the car park under Museumplein. 'During excavations of the soil for the underground polder floor, the water pressure raised the ground by 25 centimetres in just a few minutes', says the project leader from ARCADIS Bouw/Infra. And the water level simply refused to go down, no matter how much they pumped. It turned out there were still a number of holes in the water-repellent layer. The conclusion: the pit was as leaky as a sieve. ARCADIS established that the preliminary survey had been too cursory; for example, too few soundings had been carried out. But that was not the only obstacle. Also delaying the process were fears by local residents and neighbouring museums that the pile driving methods would cause too much vibration. Finally, there were a few more unpleasant surprises. The soil of Museumplein turned out to be in an even worse state of contamination than expected; there were still piles in the ground from a world exhibition at the beginning of the 20th century. A little bit of contemporary archaeology, so to speak.

9 million passengers. Moscow's metro works like clockwork. During rush hour, the wait at any of the 158 stations is never longer than 90 seconds. Might the metro be the most reliable factor in the lives of the Muscovites? Up until now, the answer is yes, although memories of several terrorist attacks are still fresh. The phenomenon of metal fatigue is also a problem, for no matter how beautifully these subterranean palaces are maintained, their rolling stock and equipment are due for refurbishment. Ironically, it was the aftermath of communism that caused the metro company's financial failures. In accordance with Soviet regulations, half of all passengers travel free. Included are not just senior citizens like Svetlana Tretyakova, but also civil servants, soldiers, the disabled, priests and young children. In all, some hundred groups are exempt from payment. Following in the footsteps of Leo Tolstoy's main character, Anna Karenina, an estimated fifteen people use the metro to commit suicide annually. The authorities are reluctant to talk about accidents and, apparently, no records are kept. It is well known that the intricate system of passageways provides shelter for more than a thousand homeless people. However distressing that may be, the metro thus remains indeed the 'palace' of the people.

Mayakovskaya metro station
Moscow, Russia

Beurstraverse
Rotterdam,
the Netherlands
De Architecten Cie/
Jerde Partnership

Treacherous soil conditions, in particular, played tricks with the Souterrain in The Hague. The Souterrain story has acquired the proportions of a soap opera, not the best thing for advocates of subterranean construction. Just a year after construction began, the contractor discovered the cause of an unstoppable leak that made the tunnel unusable. There had been insufficient preliminary investigation of an old well or stream, hidden somewhere deep under Grote Marktstraat. Every attempt to alleviate the problem, whether with grout or concrete, failed. Endless delays resulted, which is a pity, as the Souterrain, conceived by OMA, the Office for Metropolitan Architecture, approaches the emancipation of the underground in an intriguing manner, combining a traffic tunnel with shops and access to department stores, and making the Souterrain a sort of 'porch', providing comfort in the unpredictable Dutch climate. As long as they are fitted with light shafts and good ventilation, subterranean vaults could become the cathedrals of the 21st century, where, as in the past, you might seek shelter from rain and storm.

La Défense

If the Arena in Den Bosch and the Beurstraverse in Rotterdam demonstrate on a modest scale how the underground can be incorporated into shopping centres, then La Défense in Paris is still the epitome of stratified urban development on a grand scale, which, due to its size, incidentally, could only be applied *outside* the city centre, at a strategic location in the continuation of the Champs Elysées. Implantation of La Défense in the old inner city would have irretrievably destroyed that part of Paris. Although criticism of the quality of life there is increasing after twenty years – the drawback of a city is the six o'clock exodus – it is interesting to see how nearby, 19th century Neuilly has adopted an *artificial* ground level, where pedestrians are hardly aware of walking many metres above the actual surface of the earth. This effect is due to a gently rising slope with wide verges, into which so much diversity has been incorporated that the rise is imperceptible. The incidental embellishments on the raised ground level are flower beds and light wells, betraying the presence of car parks or underlying rooms in which, surprisingly enough, exhibitions can be held. Gradually, the structure approaches a highpoint – with underground architecture, too, the use of perspective is indispensable. The first of these is relatively subtle, a multicoloured fountain by the artist Arman, which appears to let its water descend into the underworld. Then, further up, the space is crowned spectacularly by a Grande Arche designed by the Danish architect, Von Spreckelsen. In other words, clever use was made in La Défense of objects by which to find your bearings at any given level, objects expressive enough to catch the eye, but not distracting in their details.

La Défense can be characterised as a two-dimensional interpretation of the ground level, with surfaces piled one on top of another, overlapping and accessible via tunnels and bridges. The monotony is relieved by a varied public area that at places offers surprising panoramas of the communal gardens below. Meanwhile, this plateau camouflages an untold amount of infrastructure, with a network of thoroughfares and a double metro station, which transports commuters to and from La Défense, lying hidden underneath.

The surface and the line

Roughly speaking, two models can be distinguished in recent developments of the ground level: a one-dimensional model with a two-dimensional variant and the linear transection of the surface versus the stacking of surfaces above ground level, of which La Défense and the Hoog Catharijne centre in Utrecht are examples. In the two-dimensional model, a comparison can be made with lasagne; at the Zuidas that shape flows over into a string of spaghetti. Typically one-dimensional is the Beurstraverse in Rotterdam, which is, ultimately, little more than a subterranean pedestrian passage under the Coolsingel, combined with access to the metro. The Coolsingel already constituted a traffic barrier between Beursplein and Van Oldebarneveltplaats, but the tunnelling also arose from economic necessity. In contrast to the large-scale selection of shops, there was a need for a more specialist, small-scale area, a centre for connoisseurs, as it were, which was increasingly and sorely missed in the rough and ready Rotterdam inner city.

No project has had as many advocates and opponents as the Beurstraverse. Its advocates – chiefly those with an economic interest and local tradespeople – praise the connecting route created between Lijnbaan and Beursplein, and are enthusiastic about the new – read Mediterranean – note introduced by Jerde, with his warm-tinted walls, which, indeed, differ considerably from the cooler format of the Lijnbaan. The choice of somewhat exotic architecture is a seductive trick Jerde has already applied in California as well as in Rotterdam. It arouses curiosity and entices the consumer to descend, always a tricky manoeuvre in the retail business, as the public is not keen on being directed downwards.

Although the success of the 'shopping drain', as it has been dubbed locally, is undeniable, since the shopping centre has also managed to attract the better shops, it puts urban development in the area in general to the test. Bluntly put, the underground programme clashes with aboveground facilities. The architects concentrated their attention so strongly on the finishing of the arcade, including security, lighting and the use of materials, that the nearby aboveground shopping area pales in comparison. There is a cultural fault line in this part of Rotterdam between the Lijnbaan and the Hoogstraat on one side and the Beurstraverse arcade on the other, which emphasises the fact that the success of underground building depends on its harmonisation with what is aboveground, and on how it is interpreted. Otherwise, the tunnels and passages end up a mere flash in the pan, soon to be discarded. This should not detract from the fact that the Beurspassage scheme has been successful in revitalising the inner city, which was a necessity given the emergence of peripheral shopping facilities.

Blaak station
Rotterdam,
the Netherlands
Harry Reijnders

The Zuidas

One-dimensional or two-dimensional? in the Zuidas, or South Axis in Amsterdam, the two options appear to flow into one another. The so-called dock model is one-dimensional; all infrastructure is placed in a closed box under the surface of the ground, with other functions, such as the Drentepark with its sports fields, the Mahlerplein and possibly offices as well, grouped directly on top. A large suburban station embraces the entire infrastructure. The task set for underground architecture in the Zuidas is very likely exemplary: simultaneity, expression and functionality fight for precedence. Simultaneity, because traffic, living and working overlap, enriched by sport and recreational activities. For the Drentepark, the architecture firm Von Meijenfeldt developed a model accommodating the AFC football fields aboveground, while the basketball courts, which prefer to operate without daylight, are located underneath. Here is an example of the intensive use of space, necessitated by the highest land prices in the Netherlands, and the need for a highly dynamic, extremely complementary environment designed for diverse income groups and users.

Unlike Potsdamer Platz in Berlin, where homogeneity has been sought at various levels, at the Zuidas expressive architecture has to balance the amorphous, monofunctional character particular to a 'work district'. The development company responsible for the Zuidas therefore looked to reputable architects, such as Toyo Ito, Rafael Viñoly and Michael Graves. Their expressive office buildings have to distinguish themselves as individual entities in an area where massiveness, expected in such a centre of high finance, predominates. Measured by volume of rail traffic, the Zuidas station is projected to be the third largest in the Netherlands, after Schiphol and Utrecht. Directional signing and landmarks, hence, are crucial both above and below ground. This will probably be the first realisation on such a large scale in the Netherlands of an integral vertical design, meaning that if you inflict a wound on the city, you have to stick a plaster over it; in this sense a smooth skin will grow between Amsterdam-South and Buitenveldert, with a finely-meshed arterial system underneath.

Government incentives

Covering motorways, tunnelling or implementing a dock model like that used for Amsterdam's Zuidas: all are part of the Dutch government's *Stimuleringsprogramma Intensief Grondgebruik* (Intensive Land Use Incentive Programme, or STIR), meant to end the massive land consumption entailed by the development of both infrastructure and industrial estates. Hence, two clear recommendations have been submitted by STIR. More roads and railway lines will have to be covered and built over or tunnelled under, while many more facilities in industrial estates will have to be sited underground or on roofs. Logically, this could include not only parking space, but also storage, logistics and other activities that do not strictly require daylight. A printers' firm in Goudriaan has taken the first step by housing its paper store and offset machines in an underground bunker. First, however, a survey had to ensure there were no leaks in that wet and marshy area in the green heart of the Netherlands.

Circulatory systems

Here is an opportunity for governments and legislators to explore relatively unknown territory. Investors should also be made aware of the appeal of this option, possibly aided by evocative images. The aestheticizing of the underground is a primary condition for overcoming potential resistance. Winy Maas, architect at MVRDV, has demonstrated how a section of motorway, in this case the northern part of the Rotterdam ring road, could be used more intensively than currently, by seeing the infrastructure as a waffle pattern, making a sharp distinction, as it were, between the functions above and below ground. Functions would be sandwiched between, under or above the roads. In this way, reasons Maas, more addresses could be added to what is now a monofunctional district. New urban boulevards could be created, along which industrial estates would be established, with several entrances to various levels. 'If you want to generate public support it is a good idea to first apply innovative concepts like this to a number of private projects. This will help political organisations overcome their initial anxiety', Maas argues. The Rotterdam model could be the proverbial first sheep. The 3D image MVRDV sketches shows similarities with the human circulatory system – and perhaps that is unconsciously the idea behind the model. Just as the human body is a system of capillaries, veins, arteries, muscles and chambers, an urban network can be similarly interpreted as a pulsating organism that lives by virtue of flow and circulation.

The 3D City is gradually beginning to emerge, a city extending above and below, with addresses at varying heights and depths. It translates the film images of Fritz Lang's *Metropolis* from the 1920s into urban reality, and makes Jules Verne's voyage to the centre of the earth seem less surrealistic. Technology is helping, too, as we descend by lifts and escalators into an underworld and even succeed in getting light to penetrate the furthest subterranean depths. There is no longer any such thing as aboveground or underground, for a new equality has been created, one we will simply have to get used to. Consider the confusion that sometimes strikes you when strolling through La Défense in Paris. Which level am I on now? And where did I leave my car?

The Netherlands: the soil is the limit

Paris, Tokyo and London prove that the 3D City already exists, partly because highly developed metro systems have provided the preconditions. In the Netherlands, with its limited underground infrastructure, another consideration could lead to the opening up of the earth. Limited space, the soft building ground and the historic heritage, combined with increasing concern for the environment, are leading inevitably to a downwards orientation. Not the sky is the limit, but the soil. Also, buildings and materials under ground level have longer life spans than those aboveground, an important financial factor. It is a question of integrating the use of underground space into urban planning, which is already happening on a cautious scale in Amsterdam's Rietlanden, where the IJ tram route has been laid under offices and residential buildings and at the same time linked to a public park. The North-South line could provide incentives for establishing functions around the stations, guaranteeing social control and safety. These could include libraries, Internet cafés, financial institutions and mega cinemas. The latest urban development designs in the Netherlands, such as those for Nijmegen, Groningen (Grote Markt), Almere and Arnhem (station and Rijnboog) show that an integral approach to above and below ground has been established, thus bringing about the emancipation of underground urban development.

The ground is there, the ideas are emerging, the ardour is awakening.

MVRDV

3 KM³ MODELS
Amsterdam

3 KM³ MODELS

Address **Amsterdam, the Netherlands**

Year **1999**

Client **Centrum Underground Bouwen,**
Gouda

Architects **MVRDV, Rotterdam**

Engineers **Ballast Nedam Engineering,**
Amstelveen

Amsterdam's hunger for space threatens its own existence. As the ground level becomes more thickly settled, the stacked surface area increases and the city expands. While underground building appears to offer new opportunities for expansion, the present underground solutions, according to the Rotterdam agency MVRDV, remain limited to incidental cases. The search for structural, integral underground forms of construction on an urban development scale has led to a number of futuristic models for the 3D City. The Gotham, Sandwich and Mine City models, conceived for the heart of Amsterdam, create new spaces under a reinterpreted ground level, making it suddenly possible to accommodate a programme with enormous potential, comparable in scope to the Zuidas in the inner city.

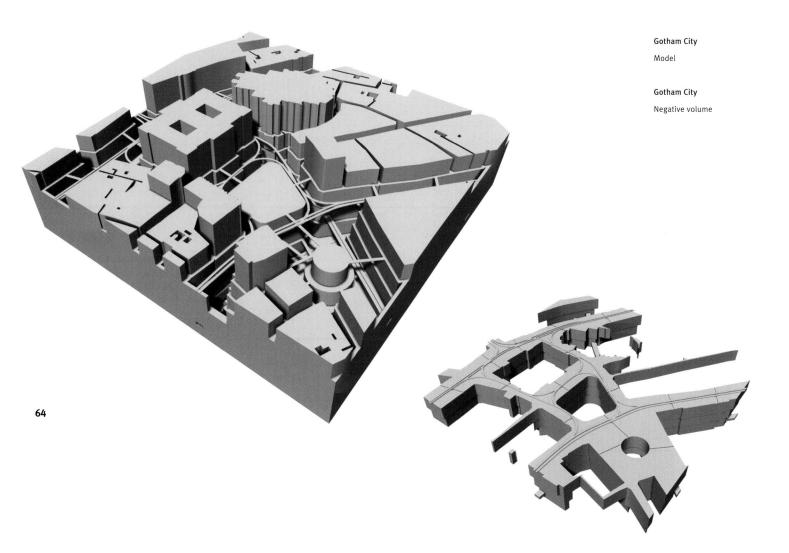

64

Gotham City

With its principle of vertical arrangement, undoubtedly inspired by Batman films, the plan would draw aboveground buildings into the earth, as if by extrusion. Deep walls around existing building units would enable them to expand downwards. Existing volumes would be increased exponentially. It would be possible to ring a doorbell on Kalverstraat and enter a head office of 100,000 m². Streets and squares would be dug up, bringing light and air deep underground. In this model, ground level no longer exists as a reference. It actually makes no difference what is above and what is below ground, since the whole programme can be positioned along a vertical axis.

Tram rails would be suspended in the air in their original positions, like the elevated metros in cities like Chicago. Pedestrians would move around several levels along the deep walls, the new facades of the underground structures. Passengers and goods would be transported vertically within the buildings and via a spiral-shaped roundabout encircling the monument on the Dam. Just as in Gotham City, accesses and connections could be created on many levels.

Gotham City
Detail of model

65

Mine City

Simulation and model

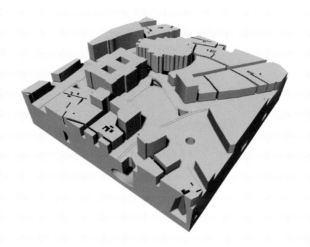

Mine City

Negative volume

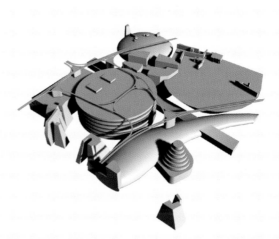

Sandwich City

In the Sandwich model, a principle of horizontal arrangement would enable various structures to be stacked, one above another. Both the ground level and the one directly beneath, containing cables, pipes, sewers and foundations, would be transformed into a constructive layer, a sort of coagulated crust. This new earth's crust, extending below building units and public spaces, would consist of a 'mega grid' of pre-stressed concrete beams, resting on a foundation of deep walls and 'mega piles,' formed in the ground. In the table-like platform constructions created by these excavations, large free spaces would be created: the city halls. These could be laid out freely, each with its own own combination of developed and undeveloped areas, of private and public spaces. Within an entirely new grid located under Amsterdam's inner city, space would be created for underground office blocks and stacked and linked volumes containing congress halls, cinemas, stadiums, shopping centres and car parks. Large and small perforations at ground level would admit light into the lower street areas. Travellers from one level to another would see a fascinating kaleidoscope of surprising interactions.

Mine City

Using an approach derived from the mining industry, large underground extensions would be carried out from ground level downwards. By freezing parts of the substratum, dome-shaped spaces could be excavated and filled with concrete constructions. The Mine City model would create a complex system of passages and voids, each with its own function: a shopping dome, a tube with traffic facilities (including the North-South line), a new Nieuwe Kerk (New Church) and a canyon for university facilities. Underground expansion would be carried out according to the same principle as expansion above ground level, where ground level remains the only reference surface. Large volumes would be added to the city almost imperceptibly. Courtyards would provide high degrees of daylight penetration. Invisible from public areas, discrete openings would provide relatively high light intensity, comparable to the light in the Pantheon in Rome.

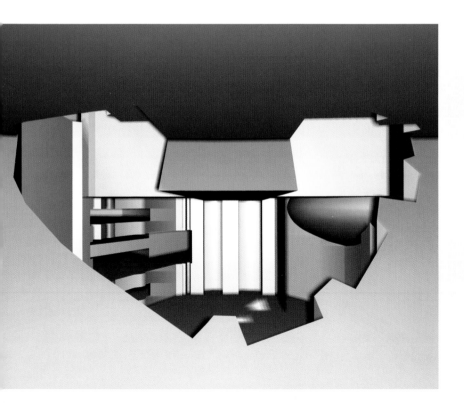

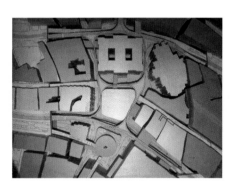

Mine City
Simulation and model

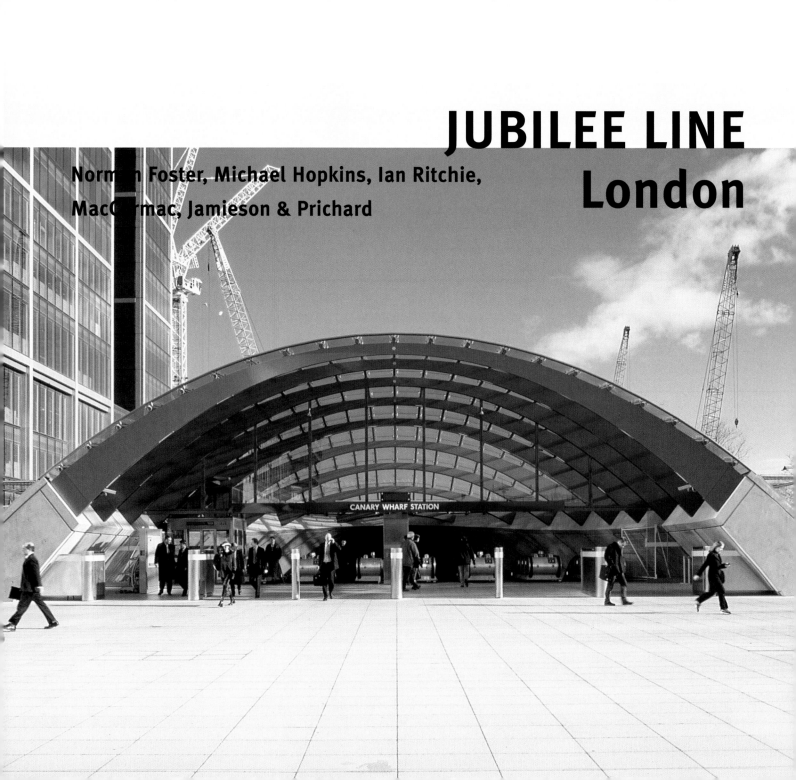

JUBILEE LINE
London

**Norman Foster, Michael Hopkins, Ian Ritchie,
MacCormac, Jamieson & Prichard**

CANARY WHARF STATION

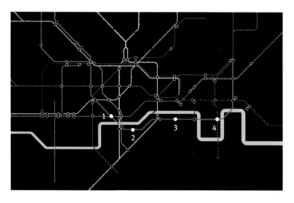

Jubilee Line

1 Westminster

2 Southwark

3 Bermondsey

4 Canary Wharf

Midway through the 20th century, investment in London's underground system came to a halt. The 'iron network', having set an example world-wide since the industrial revolution, was rapidly becoming outdated. But with the extension of the Jubilee Line, which connects North and South London diagonally, the underground has once more become a model of innovation. On the initiative of chief architect Roland Paoletti, the eleven new stations on the line were designed not by civil engineers, as is customary, but by eleven different architects. Four stations are particularly striking, constituting modern urban landmarks – worthy sequels to the great 19th-century English tradition of station construction.

Canary Wharf; Foster and Partners

The largest station on the Jubilee Line is Canary Wharf. More than 300 metres long, the station was built in a former dock. Although only three elliptical canopies protrude above ground level, you cannot miss the entrance, as these canopies are the foyers of the underground station. During rush hour, more people pass through this business station on the Thames than through busy Oxford Circus. Each day, twenty banks of escalators transport 100,000 commuters to and from the platforms, situated 27 metres below. The route is clearly defined, making directional signage virtually superfluous. Shops and administrative offices are located along the walls. The concrete columns supporting the vaulted roof take pride of place in the open, uncluttered view of the central space. Everything in this station is functional. Even lighting was installed where needed, in the escalators, for example. Safety is top priority: the platforms are separated from the rails by a barrier containing glass doors that open and shut simultaneously with those of the tube train.

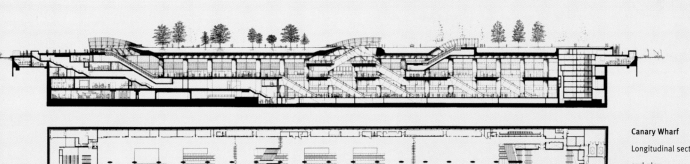

Canary Wharf
Longitudinal section
and plan

JUBILEE LINE

Underground station	**Canary Wharf**
Address	**London, Great Britain**
Depth	**27 metres**
Number of levels underground	**2**
Design	**1991-1994**
Construction	**1998**
Owner	**Jubilee Line Extension Project**
Architects	**Foster and Partners, London**
Engineers	**Ove Arup & Partners**

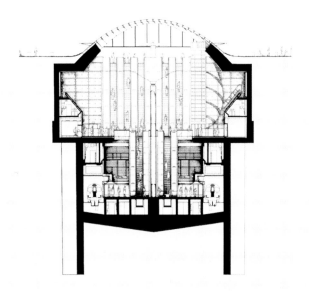

Canary Wharf
Section

Canary Wharf
Entrance

Westminster

Platform

The New Parliament Building, situated next to the world-famous Houses of Parliament, is an office building for members of parliament. The new complex includes a tube stop on the Jubilee Line, deep under ground. The tubes of the District Line and Circle Line, running diagonally under the location, made it a complicated project, not only where the design and construction were concerned, but also in terms of execution. The existing tube lines had to remain in operation during construction, and the close proximity of rather unstable historic buildings, such as Big Ben, called for extra caution. Hopkins' solution was an integral design, in which the constructions above and below ground level were designed as a single project, intersected by the existing underground lines. Surface load was transferred to the retaining walls, a kind of concrete box with a lid-like construction supported by six giant, solid pillars. Inside this box is a dramatically lit, impressive interior, where escalators, lifts, beams and columns criss-cross in space. Piranesi pales into insignificance. Here, the initial problem of angular displacement between the existing lines and the cubic volume was used to advantage.

JUBILEE LINE

Underground station **Westminster**

Address **London, Great Britain**

Depth **30 metres**

Construction time **6 years**

Construction **1999**

Owner **Jubilee Line Extension Project**

Architects **Michael Hopkins & Partners,**

London

Engineers **G. Maunsell & Partners**

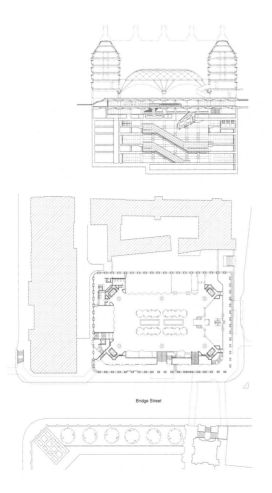

Westminster

Section and site plan

Bridge Street

JUBILEE LINE

Underground station **Bermondsey Beacon**

Address **London, Great Britain**

Depth **15 metres**

Construction time **5 years**

Design **1990-1994**

Construction **1999**

Owner **Jubilee Line Extension Project**

Architects **Ian Ritchie Architects, London**

Engineers **Ove Arup & Partners**

Bermondsey Beacon; Ian Ritchie Architects

This wonderful new station is a tribute to the synthesis of architecture and construction. The entrance is housed in a small, simple, brightly lit aboveground building. A sea of light floods in through glass walls and a slightly convex glass roof, rising above the ground. This transparent envelope transmits daylight all the way down to the level of the platforms. Columns and beams clad in stainless steel reflect the light downwards. The clearly visible, horizontal braced frame largely determines one's impression of the building, casting shadows, accentuating contrasts between light and darkness, and filtering light downwards. Ritchie gave the lower areas, in particular, a minimal finish, leaving them as rugged as possible, a play on the idea of excavation. Various aggregates, however, lend textural variety and colour to the concrete. On the upper levels, closer to public areas, the finish is more elegant. Bermondsey Station should give a boost to the surrounding area, both economically and in terms of quality of life.

JUBILEE LINE

Underground station **Southwark**

Address **London, Great Britain**

Depth **15 metres**

Construction time **6 years**

Design **1991-1999**

Construction **1999**

Owner **Jubilee Line Extension Project**

Architects **MacCormac, Jamieson**

& Prichard, London

Engineers **Aspen Group**

Southwark; MacCormac, Jamieson & Prichard

At Southwark Station, a new, eye-catching residential-style building in the mode of the 1930s welcomes passengers with a grand gesture. The other entrance is more than 200 metres away at Waterloo East station. The two flows of passengers meet underground at an elongated interim level, an attractive public area with an unusually appealing use of materials. From a central hall located at this level, passengers descend to the platforms below. This hall is a real brainwave, giving the station a focal point and uniting both sides. Spacious and conical in form, it is beautifully lit from above. By day, it is illuminated by blue-tinted daylight, in the evening by artificial cobalt-blue light. Those passengers ascending from the platforms by escalator, especially, enjoy a visual, almost mystical experience.

Manipulation for simultaneity

Interview with Floris Alkemade

Our tolerance of the adaptation of the landscape to consumption and traffic requirements appears to be slowly decreasing. Local authorities attempt to prevent the finely-meshed character of Europe's historic inner cities from being destroyed by the wide-mesh facilities needed for optimal accommodation of motorised visitors. According to Floris Alkemade at the Office for Metropolitan Architecture (OMA), the underground offers the perfect solution to this dilemma. The accepted planning practice of installing all functions at the same level leads to the enormous use of land by encumbrances and parking congestion. Taking the underground into consideration makes it possible to organise functions on top of each other. The potential result is an intense, vital city, undisturbed by heterogeneous infrastructural elements. Underground building is even the driving force behind the current updating and renewal of our cities, as here the current urban dynamic can unfold much more freely than in many an overground intervention. With relatively simple resources, we can ensure that the underground is a pleasant place to be.

For architect Floris Alkemade, the underground world is no *terra incognita*. Several years ago, he completed a research project for the Centre for Underground Building (COB) aimed at gaining more insight into the architectonic aspects of underground design assignments. Alkemade is also participating in numerous construction projects for OMA that give full consideration to underground options. Moreover, OMA sees underground building as an excellent means of realising project assignments. 'We try to combine all the elements of a programme as far as possible in our designs,' explains Alkemade. 'It makes it much easier if you can superimpose functions on top of each other, as escalators and lifts provide a fast, direct connection. Moreover, we want to offer as many options as possible to people entering a city at ground level. They should be able to go either up or down.'
For Alkemade, interrelation between levels is the most essential element of a design. He refers to such solutions by the term 'ground level manipulations'. Here, aboveground and underground are not separated by a merciless two-dimensional surface, but flow into each other, as it were, by raising and lowering, bending or folding the ground level at strategic points. 'In that way, you can bring three levels into relation with one another without visitors noticing whether they are above or below ground level', adds Alkemade. 'Ultimately, this leads to a far more intensive use of the surface area.'

Mediaeval Almere
Until recently, intensive use of space was never really an issue for the Netherlands' youngest city, Almere, lying in the middle of the vast polder landscape of South Flevoland. Instead, in order to retain its village character, they opted for a number of core areas with low-rise buildings. Now, however, Almere has outgrown village scale, and the municipality expects the number of inhabitants to rise to 240,000 by the year 2010, displacing Eindhoven as the fifth largest city in the Netherlands. Hence, the requirement for a real city centre is increasing. The municipality

commissioned OMA to design a new, compact centre, with office complexes, tower blocks and animated' zones where people can visit the theatre, a museum, the cinema, a music venue, mega stores, shops, bars and restaurants, all functions that inevitably bring with them traffic influx. 'That is one of the most essential problems in urban development at the moment', states Alkemade. 'Over the past twenty to thirty years, roads and cars have become dominant. The logic of infrastructure has grown stronger than the logic of the built-up environment; you can't stop a road just like that. But in Almere we have tried to integrate the infrastructure and the buildings by giving each its own level. At the lowest level, we are creating the ideal vehicle world, with not only parking space, but also roads and shops. Above that, we have folded a second world, the pedestrian world.' In this way, aboveground space will no longer be unjustifiably sacrificed to access roads, car parks and loading and unloading areas for servicing narrow shopping streets. 'If you situate those service functions underground', says Alkemade, 'it becomes possible to create a sort of compact, mediaeval city. In that way, you can use the area far more intensively.' A second advantage is that you can locate functions in the city that would normally have been moved to the periphery long ago, such as multiplex cinemas or music halls. 'That's how you prevent the centre from bleeding to death', says Alkemade. 'Functions that attract thousands of people a day can once more be accommodated in inner cities because the ground level doubles at crucial points, creating a perfect interrelation between the infrastructure and the programme being served. The best of the two worlds can be combined: a finely meshed inner city with functions that attract the public and an abundance of easily accessible parking spaces in just the places where the visitor wants to be.'

Making the underground more appealing

The underground as a bypass for reanimating the heart of the city. Using ground level manipulation, various programmes can be realised on a limited amount of ground. But wasn't OMA faced in Almere with the problem of the lowlands of the Netherlands of ground water at a depth of only one and a half metres? 'We did, indeed, want to test to see whether we could employ ground level manipulation in Almere', replies Alkemade. 'We took that one and a half metre depth as the basic reference point and designed the second ground level as an arched surface. Using barely noticeable slopes, we achieve a height of six metres above the original ground level. In that way, we can make underground space that rises to a free height of some six or seven metres. This spatial quality alone creates an entirely different environment than the usual oppressive car park where the ceiling is never higher than the legal minimum of 2.20 metres.' OMA has also endeavoured to make the underground space in Almere

Ground level interventions

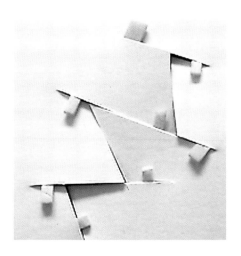

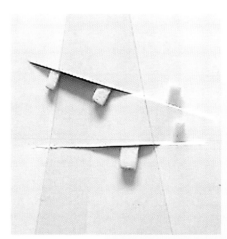

more appealing. Alkemade: 'We submerged a square to the same level as the car park, so you immediately see a square when you drive in to park, and no longer feel that you are under ground. The windows looking out at ground level and the Weerwater Lake intensify that feeling. The car park is also conveniently linked to other programmes. As the ground levels rise and fall, you can park underground and find yourself nevertheless next to the bar, the theatre and a large proportion of the shops.' Apart from good programming and spaciousness, good orientation helps make being under ground a more comfortable experience. Alkemade: 'The plan in Almere has two main routes: a vertical and a diagonal line. We lead those lines back to the car park, too, so visitors get their bearings in the same way as they do above ground. We have added vertical cores to these routes, through which daylight comes. And there are up-prints in the ceiling showing where the buildings are; you can literally read the pattern of the city plan above you from the profile in the ceiling.'

Ground level manipulation in Euralille

With ground level manipulation, infrastructure and buildings can be interrelated more subtly. In the mid-1990s, OMA already demonstrated this on a large scale in the centre of Lille, in northern France, where the arrival of the TGV had prompted drastic restructuring. This resulted in Euralille, a new business and public area, intersected by railway lines and motorways. 'The motorways aboveground and two railway lines underground with a station building above', is how Alkemade outlines the original plans. 'It was a pity that train passengers would never see the centre of the city. We therefore pushed down one corner of the triangular area between the old station and where the new one would come to stand, bringing the other corner upwards. It was as simple as that, actually. The lower part became a square and the part of the triangle that was pushed upwards was made into an enor-

84

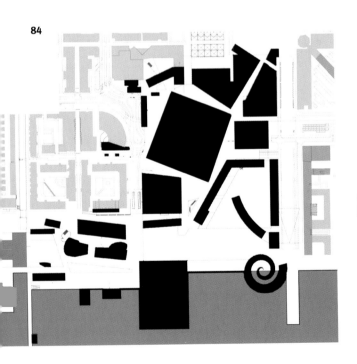

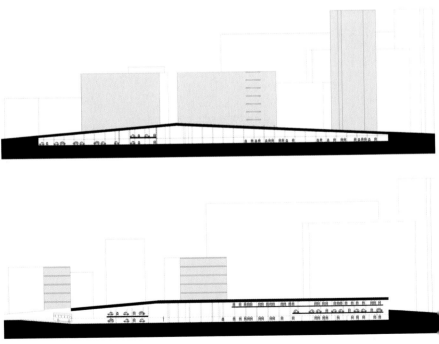

Almere

Master plan and section

mous roof, covering such facilities as shops and restaurants. We built the motorway, with car parks, at a lower level. The elements that service the area – railway and motorway – therefore no longer block the area, so the city can develop freely.' By playing with the various levels in this way, they managed to create transparency for the whole area. 'Literally', adds Alkemade. 'Despite the fact that the station is underground, passengers have a view over the entire length and in all directions: they see the square, the station itself, a deeper-situated metro station, and we even made a view through to the submerged motorway, which runs parallel with the railway line.'

Real and virtual views

For Alkemade, a view is the most essential factor contributing to making the experience of being under ground more pleasant. In his opinion, a building's design does not stop at its facade. The direct surroundings should be involved as far as possible, intensifying spatial experience. Ground level manipulation offers the solution for shallow spaces: you bring the ground level down to create a view. But how do you create a view when you have a space deep under ground? 'Then it is still possible to try and get an idea of outside space', says Alkemade. 'The underground wall is not by definition something where the world ends. With the box-within-a-box technique, you can create a kind of undefined interim space you can look out on. A wild, wet underground outside space, for example, or a subtly designed Japanese garden.' But in addition to a spatial reflection of the direct surroundings, Alkemade also sees possibilities in modern electronic media: wall-size television screens, on which an imaginary view can be projected. Technology that lies within arm's length, according to Alkemade and can simulate a plausible outside world: 'Because, in some ways, television offers a reality as large as life. Let's face it: how much time in a day do we spend looking out of the window and how long do we spend looking at a screen or watching television?'

Almere
Simulation

Singapore: the world turned upside down

In Alkemade's opinion, the need for a view is strongly culturally determined. 'We feel that you should always have a window onto the outside world at your place of work. You want to know if it's raining and if it's nice weather you want to go outside. But in the tropics, for example, it's much too hot and humid for that.' People in Singapore are not interested in what's going on outside or in a workstation with a window, Alkemade noticed when he was designing a redevelopment plan for the Singaporean Ministry of Tourism on Orchard Road, the main shopping street in the city. 'The Singaporeans try to organise things so you never have to go outside', he explains. 'All those shops are connected by enormous underground routes. An underground shopping mall, which is joined like an octopus to the entrances of large complexes. This gave shops that ended up being isolated by the infrastructure above ground a new boost.' Ground level in Singapore is therefore threatening to degrade into an area organised entirely for vehicular traffic. 'Funnily enough, Asians don't see that as at all negative. For them, the car – in Singapore almost always with air-conditioning – is actually the only way of sitting outside in comfort. So where we tend to put all the traffic underground in Europe, there it's the opposite.'

Appreciation of the underground

The appreciation Asians have for the underground is largely lacking in Europe. 'The natural train of thought is that everything above ground is beautiful and good and everything underground bad, ugly and cheap', says Alkemade. 'OMA is challenging that preconception.' The underground should never be treated like the wicked stepmother, feels Alkemade. He therefore disagrees entirely with Carel Weeber's view that, as underground buildings have no exterior, the design can easily be left to interior designers: 'You often hear that architecture is only about the recognisable form and the facade, while I believe that it's all about the way in which you organise a building. With underground construction there may be no discussion over the appearance, but I feel this brings far more essential architectural questions to the fore. The discussion therefore gains clarity and is not clouded by inappropriate esthetical arguments. You design from the inside outwards: how does a room have to function? The outside should therefore be derived from that.'

Extraordinary face

Moreover, underground spaces do have an outside, entrances and lobbies. 'The lobby is the face of an underground programme, an ambassador that tells you what is underground', says Alkemade. 'You can build an entrance in such a way that you have a view of the space under ground.' Equally interesting are cases in which an above ground building deliberately communicates a completely different message regarding the underground reality. 'The relationship between aboveground and underground is flexible, it can be manipulated', points out Alkemade, citing Disneyland as an example. 'There, they have a haunted house, a sort of spooky-looking little council house with its shutters hanging off. There are hundreds of people queuing at the entrance to get in and you think: this can't be any good. Until it turns out that the whole house is a sort of lift, which takes you to the enormous underground route. I think it's fascinating, the way a building like that communicates with the outside world.' Alkemade has an arsenal of communication media up his sleeve: 'A billboard with a logo, for example. Organisations communicate all kinds of information about themselves in a trademark, and you can make good use of that. You can dig a hole in the ground, put up an IKEA sign and everyone thinks it's an enormous project.' A design for an underground space is therefore not limited to the interior. Alkemade: 'With an underground space, to some extent, you have to take other aspects into account, and those aspects are certainly no less essential.' Call it ground level manipulation in the broadest sense of the word.

Model of multilevel underground building
Opening up for daylight and view

ARCHITECTURE

Subterranean existence Jaap Huisman

Le Carrousel du Louvre Paris

Villa Hoogerheide Hilversum

Two withdrawal rooms: Glass Temple Kyoto

Souterrain Amsterdam

SUBTERRANEAN EXISTENCE

Architectonic exploration below ground level

Jaap Huisman

In the past, people built cave dwellings of necessity, compelled by poverty or climate. This necessary evil has quite a different look in the 21st century. Crowded cities, an abundance of historical monuments, lack of space and environmental requirements: all these factors herald a new chapter in the history of underground architecture. Themes for the 21st century will be the emancipation of the car park, the discovery of the subterranean museum, and opportunities for folding, bending and elevating surfaces to create unexpected spaces. And what of the significance of light? The programmable, panoramic window is coming, which will mean that, for many activities, daylight will become unnecessary.

In autumn 2001, the world learned of the existence of yet another subterranean complex, its reputation previously restricted to a small circle, a complex of unprecedented mythical charisma. I refer to the Tora Bora cave system, in the inhospitable east of Afghanistan, presumed to have housed the most wanted terrorist in the world, Osama bin Laden.

During the era of the Soviet occupation (1979-1989), the Afghani Resistance, or Mujahadin, constructed this labyrinth of caves, tunnels and bunkers, turning a naturally occurring series of passageways into a cultural artefact, so to speak. In fact, there were already caves in the area, just as there were irrigation channels, dug over the years by farmers. They had simply not yet been linked. Even for the Afghanis, the name of Tora Bora inspired awe: it is difficult terrain, with narrow paths and ravines, where even angels fear to tread. A trip to Tora Bora approaches the suicidal – no wonder it defeated the Russians throughout their ten-year occupation. From this underground base, the Mujahadin conducted a successful guerrilla war against the occupying forces. After the Russians were ousted, it led a new life as a hideout and fort for Osama bin Laden and the Al-Qa'ida army.

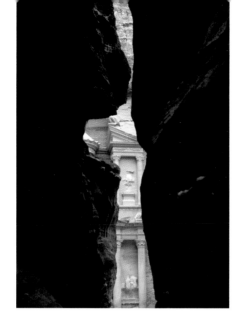

Cave tombs

Petra, Jordan

Cave dwellings

Matmata plateau, Tunisia

They set up a virtual shadow society in Tora Bora with weapons and munitions depots, drinking water basins and electricity, generated by a provisional hydroelectric power station. And, hardly unimportant in this area of extreme temperatures, a ventilation and heating system.

With such facilities, Tora Bora confirms the mythical image of an underground – and therefore invisible – habitat, like the many historical ones. Whether in the Yao Dong community in Henan, China, the excavated rocks and temples in Petra, Jordan, or the innumerable cave dwellings in Spain, France and Tunisia, humans have always felt the need to disappear beneath the ground. In the case of Tora Bora, it was a (para)military motive; elsewhere, miserable circumstances, stubborn climates or the longing for safety has driven men to inventive use of the underground. Geological conditions certainly helped: it is far more difficult to realise an underground shelter in marshy wetlands than in marl or loess.

Cinematic reality

Like Tora Bora, the Matmata plateau in southern Tunisia lies in an inhospitable area, near the Sahara. The arid plain is criss-crossed by ravines and dry riverbeds and scattered with gnawed-off mountaintops where caravans used to build their camps (*ksars*), in and under the substratum. Sometimes, you can detect human life in a rock dwelling, or an oasis, in a territory where little more than sparse thyme grows. Matmata is one of the most striking examples in the world of subterranean village communities, originally settled around the year 1500. In recent decades, an aboveground town has also been established where the inhabitants are eager to profit from the tourist attraction of the cave dwellings. Some of the scenes for Steven Spielberg's *The Temple of Doom* were shot here.

The plateau of Matmata consists of rust-brown earth, which is easily excavated, as the inhabitants have been doing for centuries, because it was a better alternative to constructing houses from bricks or adobe. There is no wood available, and scarcity of both raw materials and money motivated the inhabitants to excavate the soil. Their solution also offers a thermal advantage: the vaults are cool in summer, while in winter they offer warmth enough to shelter.

Poverty

Can we really speak of architecture in Matmata? Perhaps in one sense only. In building for themselves, people there complied with one important recommended principle for underground building: create a view. The arched vaults surround a deep, wide pit that could even conceivably be termed an atrium, which opens onto a gate in the mountain wall. Now, a hotel has been built in one of those 'pits', so tourists can see for themselves what it is like to live in the slightly moist environment. To keep out dust and moisture, the floors, which flow into wall benches, are covered with carpeting. Hardly luxurious accommodation: those at Matmata who continue to live underground are obviously the poorest of the village community. Poverty also led the inhabitants of Berg en Terblijt near the Geul Valley, in the very south of the Netherlands, to excavate the marl and set up house there at the end of the 19th century. The cave dwellings on the village street can be regarded more as pits into which people retired only to spend the night. Not far from these pit dwellings is a large system of subterranean passageways cut out of the hills, a form of accommodation found nowhere else in the Netherlands. The entrance to what is now a party centre, is still modest. But once inside you will be amazed by the labyrinth of halls and passageways where terraces have been laid out on the smoothed-out concrete. Tables stand stacked against the rough walls and lamps hang from the ceilings. The temperature is pleasant, since under-floor heating was installed. And, as it is a party cave, a professional kitchen has been set up in a large alcove. The cave's origin is less than exotic. Until thirty years ago, marl was cut into blocks here for building houses in the Geul Valley. The marl workers lived in the same humble pit dwellings along the village street.

YAWNING DEPTHS

Earth formations are architectural creations of their own right. Volcanoes, grottos and canyons convey inspiring impressions of the forces of the soil, water, wind, heat and ice.

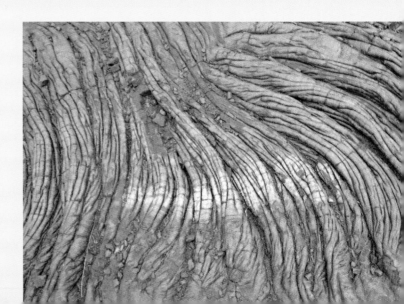

Self-preservation

In the past, going underground was a matter of survival. That is still the case in modern times, although luxury may well be a greater factor than necessity. The need is there – lack of space as a primary motivation – but luxury is manifest in the forms assumed today by underground architecture, from opulent shopping centres to cinemas, from industrial estates to museums and fancy metro stations. There is a pronounced functional divide between architecture and urban development. Functions definitely requiring aboveground sites because they need light and air will be accommodated, while increasingly, anything that can be will be built under surface level. As a consequence, new philosophies need to be developed for architecture, linked to new typologies. The first hesitant signs are already there: noise barrier homes, underground museums and shopping centres and the elevated ground level used for car parks (the 'Ezelsoor' in Amsterdam's Museumplein) or visitors' centres (De Hoep in Castricum, NL). The modern car park seems to be generating a new building typology, in any case, as it is already being combined with supermarkets or art galleries (there are various examples in the US).

Considering how separate these two worlds once were, the merging of the visible surface with the invisible world below is extraordinary, to say the least. In the past, the invisible appealed to the imagination strongly enough to generate innumerable myths. In Delphi, the high priestess Pytha sat above a crevasse in the earth's crust, while vapours emerging from the abyss nourished her prophetic spirit. The roman catacombs, the accommodations for slaves and wild animals, the baths, the first rudimentary sewers and the necropolises: all demonstrate that ground level has long since yielded to create a shadow counterpart of the world above.

De Hoep

Castricum,

the Netherlands

Min 2 Architecten

In the 20th century film, especially, adopted the underworld as a theme, as a source of the incomprehensible and the criminal, synonymous with evil. Ironically, Afghanistan's Tora Bora confirms the prejudice Hollywood promoted about the underworld. Even worse, even if Tora Bora had never existed, Hollywood would certainly have invented it as soon as the trauma of 11 September, 2001 had been assimilated.

This archetypal idea of the invisible seen in films is at odds with changing economic reality. Not evil itself, but certain necessary evils, such as the infrastructure that keeps our cities accessible, must be housed underground. Shopping centres and industrial estates, for example, which we treat as blots on the landscape, and are ideally hidden away. Not to mention car parks and wastewater purification plants, like the one in Dokhaven in Rotterdam. The relocation of this plant underground not only has the advantage of reducing odors as far as possible, it also enables it to be incorporated into a residential area.

Metro

When did contemporary exploration under ground level begin? At the end of the 19th century, probably, with the construction of metros in such metropolises as New York, London and Paris. It seems clear that, at least initially, improvements in transport efficiency, facilitated by new discoveries like the lift and the escalator, made underground construction necessary. Now, almost a century later, we can see how this need has grown. Metro stations are being combined with shopping centres, offices and car parks and the surface has not only been torn open, but also divided into levels. 'Lasagne architecture' has won a place in the metropolises, in the form of La Défense in Paris, Hoog Catharijne in Utrecht and in a complete subterranean complex in Montreal. In the Hague, an underground network of tram rails and tunnels is also gradually growing, in competition with the visible traffic system.

If the entrances to the earliest examples of metro architecture were recognisable beacons, tempting passengers to descend to the platforms (the most beautiful examples being Hector Guimard's art-nouveau porches), then modern metro buildings are also surface symbols, hinting at the traffic below. Guimard unmistakably set the tone for a major aspect of underground architecture. Anyone wanting to inform people that something important is happening below had better announce it in no uncertain terms. The choice of

expressive architecture is therefore obvious; otherwise an entrance to the underground will remain unnoticed amid the street scene.

In the 1970s, the architects of the Amsterdam metro won prizes for their sturdy, stepped buildings on
Wibautstraat and Weesperstraat, heavy concrete constructions that, thirty years later, seem more like obstacles
than enticements. Today's architects often opt for transparent entrances. In this context, the glass porches of
the Lyon metro, designed by Jourda & Perraudin, are more subtle, although some of their figurative aspects
seem debatable: they spread their wings like giant dragonflies above the entrances, creating visual discord on
the surface. On the other hand, this solution is understandable, as the glass creates visibility, at some stops,
from the threshold all the way to the platforms, drawing the metro into the city as part of a living organism.
True enough, the same was also achieved in Bilbao's metro by other means, thanks to Norman Foster's elegant
glass street level probosces, allusions to the high-tech ambience inside the stations, with their abundance of
glass and stainless steel – sophisticated materials reflecting light into unexpected places. A shift in focus is
detectable in metro architecture: from a logistical transport system, it has developed into a type of accommodation, enticing people to stay underground longer than a hundred years ago.

This could be seen as a minor revolution in perceptions of the metro. They are multifunctional, lighter and
better organised, all psychological ingredients that make spending time underground more pleasant, to such
a degree that you are hardly aware of being deprived of direct sunlight.

Lobby

Experience shows that to make a metro system feasible, clearly marked entrances are necessary, preferably
ones that are psychologically and aesthetically enticing. In front of Rotterdam's Blaak station, an inclined disc
symbolises the train station below; the roof functions like a lens, transporting light downwards. This station
foyer may not be a lobby in the traditional sense of the word, but it is so in the modern sense, i.e., a sheltered
place on the surface, providing indications of underground activities. In the subterranean museums and the new
generation of car parks, the entrance has grown into a transparent 'box' whose brightness seeks to compensate
for the dusk of 'the shades'. The architecture has to be inviting – and it is, too, as more and more effort is being
spent on making entrances look like more than simply a ticket office, a counter or a place of shelter. The foyers
of the car park for Amsterdam's Museumplein take the forms of a restaurant, souvenir shop and public lavatories (they are so wonderful, in fact, that they have won a prize) and in Laakhaven, in the Hague, decorative

Metro entrance
Lyon, France
Jourda & Perraudin

Metro entrance
Paris, France
Hector Guimard

Metro entrance
Bilbao, Spain
Foster and Partners

glass towers accentuate the public area. In Forum des Halles, in Paris, a lobby can have an additional function, for example as an entrance to a playground or a small conservatory. The intention is clear: in buildings serving simply as 'limbos' leading to the 'real building' underground, a feeling of social safety is essential.

Elevated ground level

Lobbies are tiny pimples on the surface, signs of underground existence, but sometimes the whole surface 'moves'. The manipulation of ground level appears to be the remedy for revitalising parts of the inner city and making western European urban centres attractive. These operations are prompted by such factors as new forms of infrastructure, including high-speed trains, lightrail and metros. For the area around the station in Lille, the Office for Metropolitan Architecture worked out various schemes for providing relief in a flat area. And relief, the diversification of the silhouette, is the classical way of giving a city an urban character. The suburbs of Lille lacked such urban reference points, just like Almere, in the Netherlands, which is oppressed by a flatness, causing monotony and a lack of orientation.

Can ground level be modelled to create organic links between urban development and architecture? It can, reasoned OMA, by making incisions in the flat surface – simple, contrary, curved, linear – or intersecting it with straight or zigzagging lines and T-junctions. And there is a third option, that of lowering, raising, folding or turning back the ground level and then combining those variations with intersecting routes. In Euralille, site of the junction of the TGV, of congress centres and a shopping mall, those theories culminated in an enormous, triangular, upward-sloping roof, under which run internal routes leading train passengers logically to Lille's old city centre.

As mentioned earlier, the modernist city suffers from a certain flatness, which means that potential points of reference are neglected, especially if the architecture is also homogeneous. Referring to Almere, current Dutch government architect Jo Coenen once remarked that the modern city centre, in particular, needs reference points that persist in memory, whether monuments, points of emphasis, or even a certain atmosphere in a square or tower. Cities that fail to make lasting impressions fail to last themselves. People visit them once, never to return. That was a consideration for the Almere's town council when it decided in the mid-1990s to radically reverse its policy, following an impulse to finish the centre in a spectacular manner. To that purpose, a corner between the town hall and Weerwater lake has deliberately been left fallow.

Laakhaven car park
The Hague,
the Netherlands
Atelier Pro

Paradox

Rem Koolhaas had the right touch to complete the composition, for he is oblivious to historical ballast. He is adding perspective to the flat pancake of Almere by means of an elevated surface that rises in the direction of the Weerwater, the city's central lake. There will also be some fraying of the selvages and tearing up of the existing, rather skimpy cut of the centre – like an ice flow raising itself above the surface of the ice and catching the sunlight.

The solution is ingenious in its very simplicity. Almere is trying to create an urban silhouette, something it has always lacked. The artificial slope provides a 'natural' panorama of the lake and the polder behind it. Last but not least, an interesting underground space will be created. In this case, underground is a relative term: the existing ground level will be covered by the sloping roof. Almere is not going downwards.

Urban architects have already likened the space under the elevated surface to a cathedral, although unjustifiably, as they themselves admit, since the many columns will slightly counteract the impressive effect. Nevertheless, this high area provides space, and even a place of honour for the car, so often discouraged or even banned in many cities. In the meantime, a bus lane also runs through the space, which, although Almere's main artery for surface level public transport, is not a barrier like the Coolsingel in Rotterdam. Finally, a department store and shops will be setting up under the inclined surface, in accordance with a pattern devised by the French architect, Christian de Portzamparc. He picked up the theme of intersecting axes, but has staggered them in relation to each other at the point where the roads cross. His reasoning? This is precisely what gives a mediaeval city its charm; the unexpected squares at crossroads and streets whose ends you can never quite see. This generates excitement in a city and encourages you to come back to learn its secrets. Such variation is not simply decorative; it is also a way of finding your bearings, even underground.

Almere appears to embody a paradox of subterranean construction, for the city is not actually burying facilities underground, but adding a complex layer to the centre, creating an illusion of underground architecture. This is combined with elements of urban development reminiscent of classical Italy, such as slopes, shifts in perspective and, above it all, towers protruding from the sloping surface. All in an attempt – which makes the task so interesting – to create a synthesis of urban development and architecture, of the one-dimensional and the multidimensional.

Euralille
Lille, France
Office for Metropolitan
Architecture

Car park
Arnhem, the Netherlands
UN Studio

Car park

The prominent significance of the car park in Almere already indicates that car parking has been freed from its wicked stepmother image. Here, as mentioned earlier, a new building typology emerges. It has graduated from wasted space to being an urban reception hall, with attention paid to pleasant lighting and art on the walls to help motorists get their bearings. The car park integrated below the town hall and library complex in The Hague is an architectural complex perceived as a unity. It demonstrates an innovation in the role of the car park and the car in the city. In Breda and Arnhem, the concept of the integral car park has been taken even a step further. Architects are among the few people capable of bridging the gap between infrastructure and urban development: Rem Koolhaas in Breda, Ben van Berkel in Arnhem. For the car park under Breda's Chassé park, the architect opted for an ingenious play of lighting and materials, with illuminated speckled basalt resembling quartzite in a coalmine. At the station in Arnhem, Van Berkel folded the parking levels under each other. By creating an expressive, undulating vault, he ensured that daylight was still able to penetrate into the bottom of the car park, a break with the traditional underground 'box'.

Countryside

Clear motives prompted Almere, a modern municipality, to introduce stratification into its flat centre. It will help improve quality of life, which depends on two elements of contemporary planning: accessibility and diversity. But what significance can underground architecture have in the open countryside of the Netherlands?
The answer is economy. In this case, economy means not cold calculation, but the increasing need to save the horizon in the lowlands. Since the Netherlands does not have an abundance of open countryside, what little it does have must be conserved.

One may draw a parallel with Japan, which admittedly must contend with a space problem entirely different from that of the Netherlands, as not marshy soil, but volcanic mountains leave no more than a tenth or so of the country's total surface area for development. Here, architects turn to the underground especially for facilities easily accommodated there, such as – once again – infrastructure (stations, shopping centres) and museums.

Past and present

On the island of Kyushu, Tadao Ando built the Forest of Tombs Museum, which one might call emblematic of underground architecture in the open field. Ando's choice of an underground solution seems consistent with his typical approach. Favoring the use of smooth concrete walls, his designs favour grooves in the surface of the ground, leading visitors via slopes into the depths, where unexpected perspectives have been created using openings as visual frames. His Museum of Tombs treats its theme, the age-old crypts of the Futago-zuka culture, so compellingly that any other architectural solution for this place becomes unimaginable. The landscape of the southernmost island of Japan is dark green, with enchanting slopes that swell unnaturally in places. Underneath lie the tombs with their rock drawings and graves. Several tumuli were copied for the museum and placed under a cavernous vault, accessible only by a long, spiral staircase. Ando asks us to take enough time to descend into history, while the way back is correspondingly short, via a straight staircase; having absorbed the impressions, we quickly return to present-day reality. As with a metro station, a beacon is needed to attract the attention of passers-by to the underground. Ando has limited himself in this landscape to two slender towers – almost watchtowers – and a long wall, each full of symbolism. The towers, with their glass tops, are like a gesture to the heavens, catching light and feeding it downwards. The wall shelters the treasures from the 'evil' of the outside world. Ando attempts to connect past and present, with the ground level as the dividing line.

In Europe, Ando has shown respect for the South German landscape with his Vitra conference building in Weil am Rhein. While his colleague, Frank O. Gehry, pulled out all the stops with a lavish, sculptural building, Ando restricted himself to a pavilion that zigzags around the cherry trees like a bolt of lightning. Here is a synthesis between an almost contemplative architecture and the landscape, receding or approaching in mutual respect. The heart of the pavilion is a large court, almost a pit, clad with the concrete plates so characteristic of Ando's work. With an unexpected view of the cherry trees, Ando has reversed top and bottom, as it were. More than that: his architecture shows that a pavilion can be an extended lobby, in balance, where spatial perception is concerned, with the underground rooms.

Dunes and woodland

While Ando restricts his architectonic interventions to the landscape, it is increasingly common in the Netherlands to use the landscape itself as a tool. There are numerous examples from the 1990s, ranging from noise barrier homes to grass roofs. Maarten Min's Visitors' Centre at De Hoep in Castricum is suggestive of a dune; Wim Quist's museum in Scheveningen does the opposite, for it is concealed *in* a dune. De Hoep is an elevated continuation of the woodland and dune landscape, with a roof of sedum and an entrance shaped like an enormous sewage pipe – a specimen of underground building aboveground. The Beelden aan Zee Museum is a cultural air-raid shelter, offering refuge from the onslaught of the world at large, inviting visitors to concentrate on the sculptures, displayed on plinths in perfect peace and quiet.

Both projects are set in the middle of stunning scenery, and both fulfil the need for a view of the world outside; at the *moment suprême*, Quist's window offers visitors a panoramic view of the North Sea just as Isaac Israels might have painted it, while Min's large windows at De Hoep present vegetation almost like a series of still-lifes in a natural history museum. Contrasts between enclosed space and light apertures are sharply accentuated in each case, allowing both light and intimacy to be experienced all the more strongly. That contrast is one of the trump cards of subterranean construction, whose aesthetics consist primarily of modesty, or rather, reverence for nature.

In Castricum and Scheveningen, therefore, you could say that landscape dictates architecture. In both cases, ground level had to be conserved, or at least left free of conspicuous architecture. In Scheveningen, a further contributing factor was that the museum was allowed a place in the sea defences, one of the most sacred locations in the Netherlands. It also nestles under the Von Wied pavilion, a favourite spot of the Dutch royal family at the beginning of the 20th century. Here, the architect had to handle the project with kid gloves, working among the sand reeds with respect for both history and ecology.

Forest of Tombs Museum

Kumamoto, Japan

Tadao Ando

Hollow Road

For many years, a sign reading 'Aluvium Industrial Estate' has stood near the Dutch-German border area of Bocholtz. It recalls a dream that will probably never come to fruition, for a tiny indigenous population of wild

hamsters has thrown a conservational spanner into the works, unaware of stymieing one of the most interesting examples of subterranean construction in the open countryside. The landscape is like that of Kyushu, Japan, undulating and almost un-Dutch in its hilliness, with unspoiled vistas. This purity, however, has to compete with the area's economic potential, very popular with Dutch distribution companies. Trucks come and go or stand in the big car parks.

If underground building is justified anywhere, then it is here, where it could preserve the virgin landscape. Ashok Bhalotra of Kuiper Compagnons had an ingenious plan for this hill. Like Ando, he pictured a groove in the landscape that provides access to a partially underground industrial estate, hardly warranting the term 'high-profile location'. Any attempt to camouflage industrial estates is praiseworthy, given that, in the 1990s, the sides of many motorways rapidly silted up with unattractive, anonymous boxes.

But more than hamsters prevented the execution of this underground industrial estate; there was also uncertainty concerning planned water drainage via the artificial 'hollow' road. Limburg's hilly landscape had already paid the price in the 1990s for erosion caused by deforestation and farming practices applied due to land consolidation. For this reason, any new intervention is considered very carefully. Even though it remained on paper, the design took account of ecological factors. The vast amounts of energy consumed by such industrial estates could be reduced. Moreover, the excavations and the water transport meant that a logical circuit of rainwater and wastewater could be installed. Bhalotra had a varying, excavated environment in mind, in which companies would be connected to each other via bridges and large complexes would be provided with light from sunken courtyards. There would be a division between buildings contributing to the estate's image and more service-oriented ones. Bhalotra planned to set the former in the foreground, with the latter concealed behind them.

Noise barrier homes

In order to remain unspoiled itself, the landscape may even dictate the architecture. Sometimes, however, there is no alternative to a landscaping element, since otherwise, building at a specific location would be out of the question. The Netherlands therefore increasingly tends to build homes *in* the noise barriers, homes that would

Vitra Conference Pavilion
Weil am Rhein, Germany
Tadao Ando

101

Aluvium Industrial Estate

Heerlen-Aken,

the Netherlands

Kuijper Compagnons

Limburg Archives

Maastricht,

the Netherlands

RGD / Marc van Roosmalen

otherwise have had no chance at all, due to traffic noise from a motorway or railway line. Experiments in this area were performed on Tilburg's Delmerwieden housing estate, and the same construction type was also chosen at the Heerlen-Aken industrial estate, in the form of 'underland homes'. But these experiments are not (yet) entirely free from troubles. The key question is how to permit daylight to penetrate the back of the houses, and how a sensible relationship can be established between homes and public areas. This type of accommodation is defensive, a row of houses that shuns the dominant public area. Another uncertainty is the expansion of the layer of earth on the roof when it becomes waterlogged and then freezes. In Tilburg, the solution was to install drainage between the earth and the concrete construction. But there's more: would inhabitants feel buried alive? Or instead, sheltered from wind and weather? Only time will tell which perception prevails.

Under the pavement

The underground beckons. Under the pavement is not a swamp, but a beach, fantasised the popular Dutch author, A.F.Th. van der Heijden, in his book, *Toothless Time*. Underground exploration is especially tempting in areas with extreme climate differences or lack of space. And anyone daring to take that step knows that public space is the winner, as squares and parks are created that are liberated from traffic. That is the advantage in Cologne, where the Cologne Philharmonic concert hall was built under the street, and a continuous square created between the station and the banks of the Rhine. It is also the advantage of the Vrijthof in Maastricht and for Museumplein in Amsterdam. At Mariënburg, in Nijmegen, development is possible at various levels, and a dead corner of the city has now been brought to life. The expressive architecture helps entice visitors from other parts of the city, which pale into insignificance after the metamorphosis at Mariënburg. Such measures only succeed when conditions above and below ground are in balance, and when people below are provided with light and air from above, and people above are aware of how lively things are underground. Sight and light are the keys, a balance apparently secured on the premises of Delft's Technical University, where Mecanoo completed the university library at the end of the 1990s. Here, several principles of good subterranean construction were adhered to. At ground level stands a glass cone, indicating the presence of the building below, while casting light into the library in such a way that books are not damaged. In a university district filled with concrete, the grassy slope has been developed into an oasis of green.

Views

Once, I happened to stay at the Lowry Hotel in Manchester, England. It was way over my budget, but I had no desire to look any further. Also, it was to be a short night, since my flight the following morning departed early. Perhaps we could negotiate over the price of the room? Well, not exactly, said the receptionist, but there was another solution. There were several rooms without views, which were much cheaper. I simply couldn't imagine it. A room without a view? She explained that they were situated in awkward corners between the inner courtyard and the lift shaft and could therefore be seen as an architectonic miscalculation. When I entered my room, I saw how the mistake had been solved. A large curtain had been hung against one wall, suggesting a window. I pulled it aside and saw before me the nocturnal panorama of a metropolis. A room with a virtual view of a fantasy city. The only thing missing was the city noise, but they had even thought of a windowsill and a window box of mother-in-law's tongues.

Are daylight and views really so important when a hotel is only used to sleep in? Apparently not. And let's face it, enclosure and absence of daylight are characteristic of underground architecture. For many functions or activities, daylight is irrelevant or even undesirable. A basketball court is better off under the ground, and the same is true for cinemas, theatre auditoria, garages, depots, archives, control rooms and ice complexes. One of the most interesting experiments in the latter category was the construction of an ice hockey stadium in the Norwegian town of Gjovik, for the Olympic Winter Games in 1994. In place of a closed box that would mar the vulnerable mountain landscape, a stadium housed in hollowed-out rock prevented such aesthetic damage and made it possible to produce a climatologically pleasant and spatially imposing stadium.

On balance, lack of light is no longer a pressing reason for rejecting underground architecture. Technology comes to our aid, now that light intensity can be raised to more than 2,500 lux, enabling underground conditions to vie with daylight. In some Japanese underground shopping centres, the designers are even able to manipulate light so that consumers perceive its daily fluctuations, and even the influence of the seasons. Further developments of the artificial panorama can also be expected – see the example of the hotel in Manchester – in the form of the flat, wide projection screen, effacing the distinction between real and filmed nature. Anyone spending relatively short periods in enclosed spaces could live with a simulated view, perhaps even ordering snowflakes in August.

An interim solution

Still, the best interim solution is often a combination of natural and artificial light. When the University of Limburg decided to set up its main building in the heart of Maastricht, in a mediaeval cloister with 19th-century wings, architect Jo Coenen successfully proposed the following plan. He converted the basement into the main space, connecting it to the new underground auditorium below the garden, thus killing two birds with one stone. He retained the historic complex of buildings and gave it back to the city as a living organism. Visitors aboveground would never suspect the existence of the new lecture hall on the premises, a stone's throw from the River Jeker, so naturally is it incorporated into the slope. Inside, the experience is exactly the opposite. There, the hall appears as a shell-shaped auditorium, with light entering through slits distributed around the hall's circumference. Underworld and upper world trade places as Coenen pulls strings like a puppeteer, benefiting both worlds. On the way to the hall, the raw foundations of concrete formwork are visible, on top of which the cloisters were set in the 20th century, and a dark shaft leads into the auditorium, which indeed feels as though it were situated under ground. And so it is, albeit with an unexpected view of the garden.

Further up the same street, architect Marc van Roosmalen repeated the principle of light slits that admit daylight, casting it onto centuries-old walls. A narrow atrium on one side of the old ambulatory brings the vaults of the new Limburg Archives, built in 1994-1995, to life. Here, too is a cluster of old buildings, including the 14th-century Franciscan church, with its monastery garden. Three levels down, beneath this square, is the archive space, anchored in a concrete bunker intended to provide protection from the excess water seeping from the River Jeker during winter floods. Van Roosmalen applied the 'tip of the iceberg principle': under the

UNDER FIRE

Time and again, fear of destruction throws mankind back to the earth. In the event of danger, people stretch themselves out flat against the ground, driven by the necessity for self-preservation. The greater the fear, the stronger the urge to lie prostrate on the ground or disappear into it. Put differently, we feel safer within the earth than on top of it. The trench is the embodiment of the architecture of fear.

In the Middle Ages, people took cover from enemies behind earthen walls. Danger was predictable, at least in the sense that it always came overland; only the direction of approach was unknown. In those days, a good view could be a matter of life or death. Nowadays, however, such bastions are chiefly decorative: geometry and symmetry, once chosen for efficiency, are now perceived as the attributes of 'Land Art.'

Once technology had advanced to the degree that danger could be expected from any direction, even from the air, a new kind of 'fear city planning' developed. People felt safer underground. Invisible to the enemy, they endured the inconveniences of air-raid shelters and bunkers. The former Soviet Union has now revealed the kind of secret 'cities of fear' this could produce. In the 1960s and 70s, an entire subterranean shelter city was built near Moscow for 10,000 party officials, with cinemas, theatres, luxurious apartments and a special metro line to the city centre. A similar subterranean city was also built under Beijing around the same time.

Such underground cities were designed, not with current fears in mind but in anticipation of future threats. The Maginot line, built by the French before World War II, Cu Chi in South Vietnam, an extraordinary and vast network of tunnels extending from Ho Chi Minh city to the Cambodian border, and the 'Moscow Escape City' were all built in the belief they would afford protection in imminent catastrophes – none of which, incidentally, actually occurred.

small but monumental apex lies an enormous underground mountain of facilities. Here is a clue to the inevitable fate of historic monuments, which can only survive by making their undergrounds available, ensuring them new functions. Now and again, however, they also reveal unexpected glimpses of their origins. The Archives offer a marvelous passage from 14th-century marl and bluestone to glass, steel and concrete. It would hardly be exaggerated to call this the reverse of Orpheus' voyage: from past to present.

In both the Archives building and the university, light is used as a spatial tool, which also does more justice to historic buildings.

Orientation and contemplation

In public complexes, light aids orientation. In the Carrousel du Louvre in Paris – the shopping centre connected to the museum entrance – a hanging pyramid, or light cone (actually the mirror image of the pyramid above ground) supports orientation. Light, sight and view: these are the three basic conditions for laying out an underground space, for they promote identification and therefore feelings of safety. People like to understand their surroundings cognitively and, at the same time, experience a wealth of impressions. Hence their preference for historic environments, which offer a natural diversification. In the underground, naturally, such differentiation is also important, but even more so is order and organisation. Paris' Forum des Halles presents those components in an ingenious manner, leading users through interior gardens, atriums and past a swimming pool, where they experience differences in height and nuances in colour, all of it intended to prevent boredom. Spatial variety, in particular – the route leads through spaces that are large, then intimate, then vast, and finally small and cosy

Fort McHenry
Baltimore, Maryland, USA

– helps users forget being underground altogether. In Japan, such spaces feature two additional elements: the simulation of daylight and the injection of scents.

Indirect light can, after all, contribute to a contemplative atmosphere. The Temppeliaukio church in Helsinki raises the question whether the underground might not be ideal for places of worship, for reflection, far from the madding crowd. The church was hewn from rock, and lies like a meteorite in the middle of a residential area. In the round nave, purple cushions on the pews form the only (but very effective) colour accents against grey granite and wooden balustrades and furniture. The windows, the wonder of Temppeliaukio, are situated around the ceiling like an aureole, and admit daylight which tinted glass then projects onto the walls like a rainbow. It is a sophisticated arrangement, because in Finland, the sun lies very low for much of the year. In this church, too, the architecture shows how expressiveness need not rely on elaborate style, but can result from the skilful use of light and indigenous materials.

Lack of direction

In both mythology and Hollywood film, the underworld is the seat of all evil; in contemporary urban development it is simply a necessary evil. Cities, which of necessity utilise every square centimetre of space, have two directions to choose from: up or down. Improved technologies in construction, lighting, ventilation and acoustics have shown that the underworld is no longer off limits. Without noticing, we are spending greater and greater periods of time in sunless halls and centres, whether they be concert halls, cinemas, tunnels or metros. And there is no way back. The air-raid shelter has lost its privilege; there is a general jostling for place underground. After all, what is the alternative? Should we decide the earth has nothing to offer surface level urban development, ground level would be the loser, the open countryside would be doomed to disappear, the city threatened with asphyxiation. That is the paradox of underground building: it is the only way to let the world breathe. The potentially rich underground is also infinite. If no boundaries are defined, then the result is unrestricted architecture, eating its way through the body of Mother Earth like a tapeworm. The cellars of Rem Koolhaas' Villa Floriac allow a glimpse behind the scenes. Construction photographs show a labyrinthine pattern of rooms, like those seen in the excavations at Pompeii. Hierarchy and order are missing, since they play hardly any role in underground building culture. The temptation to knit rooms and passageways into each other is great – look at the disorganised cave complex of Tora Bora.

Lack of direction, resulting in amorphous architecture, is the greatest threat to underground building. At the same time, freedom of direction – a subtle difference – is the great challenge.
The more disorganised the pattern becomes, the more often the spectres of social insecurity and irrational fear rear their ugly heads. And the underground has only recently banished them.

Villa Floriac
Bordeaux, France
Office for Metropolitan
Architecture

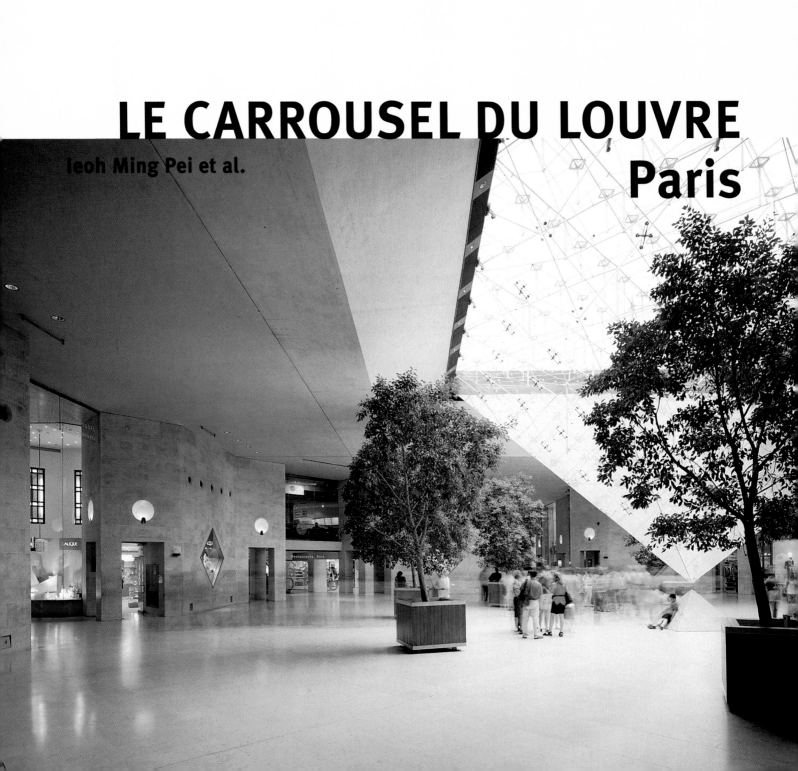

LE CARROUSEL DU LOUVRE
Paris

Ieoh Ming Pei et al.

LE CARROUSEL DU LOUVRE

Function	**shopping centre**
Address	**99, rue de Rivoli, Paris, France**
Construction volume	**1,700,000 m³**
Facade surface area	**90,000 m²**
Depth	**14 metres**
Number of levels underground	**2**
Construction time	**4 years**
Initiative	**1981**
Design	**1988-1992**
Construction	**1990-1993**
Client	**The French government**
Architects	**I.M. Pei, Macary, Duval, New York**
Engineers	**Sogelerg, Serete**

Le Louvre

1 Arc de Triomphe du
  Carrousel
2 Cour Napoléon
3 Cour Carrée
4 Palais Royal
5 Musee d'Orsay
6 Seine river

Almost immediately after its erection in 1988, the transparent pyramid in the inner courtyard of the Louvre museum, designed by architect Ieoh Ming Pei, was acknowledged as a landmark. This 'light-hearted' symbol of modernity blended well with the solid background of the museum complex, and the efficient underground entrance was subsequently extended to include a large-scale shop and auditorium complex: Le Carrousel du Louvre. The overall plan is consistent with the philosophy according to which French public art treasures are a part of world culture – although the design also jars slightly with that philosophy, since, for many, Le Carrousel is synonymous with the commercialisation of art.

Until recently, the Ministry of Finance in Rue Rivoli entirely hid the Louvre museum. Busy traffic further increased that isolation. The Cour Napoleon, one of the Louvre's courtyards, was used by personnel as a car park, making access to the museum by car virtually impossible. Now that the 'Grand Louvre' has been completed, visitors can leave their cars in the spacious underground car parks of Le Carrousel. Part of the traffic flow has also been diverted underground around the Louvre, pedestrian subways have been added, and a metro stop has been integrated into the plan. The nine-hectare complex, sited under the gardens between the two wings of the museum, links various parking levels and a metro station to the museum via attractive shopping arcades.

Visitors to the Louvre can stroll for hours in Le Carrousel through regal, seven-metre high shopping streets. The famous glass pyramid forms a familiar entrance to both museum and shopping centre. From the underground inner courtyard, a long, east-west axis leads ultimately to the car parks. The design and use of materials for the shopping complex fit in well with the architecture of the museum entrance. All shops have been laid out identically and, thanks to strict advertising regulations, project a uniform image. Roughly at mid-point, the avenue is interrupted by a small upside-down glass pyramid, a witty reminder of its famous aboveground counterpart. On sunny days, it reflects all the colours of the rainbow. Certain measures create the feeling of being outside; the lighting generates a kind of accelerated perspective, making the space seem even higher and lighter, while the ventilation has been designed to produce an occasional breeze, and even noticeable changes in temperature.

France's safety regulations for public areas are unusually strict. For underground public areas they are even more stringent. In the Grand Louvre, concealed steel ladders automatically appear in case of emergency, connecting Le Carrousel directly with the surface. The entire area is monitored and controlled in a number of ways, and all this information is registered and partly interpreted by a 'self-learning' programmed computer.

This ambitious project cost 150 million Euro. To make the entrance area of the Louvre cost-effective, Le Carrousel needs to attract a host of activities. Four auditoria with flexible floors, walls and lighting consoles can accommodate fashion shows, concerts and conferences. A range of fifty shops, with the focus on expensive clothing and art, forms a pleasant surrounding for these sidelines.

VILLA HOOGERHEIDE
Hilversum

Jo Crepain

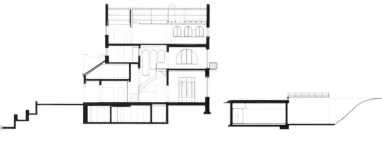

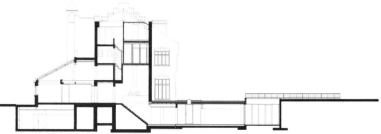

Villa Hoogerheide

Cross-section and

longitudinal section

VILLA HOOGERHEIDE

Function **office**

Address **Ceintuurbaan 2, Hilversum,**

the Netherlands

Construction volume **2,000 m³**

Facade surface **3,300 m²**

Floor surface **840 m²**

Depth **3 metres**

Number of levels underground **1**

Design **1998**

Construction **1999**

Client **Johan Matser Project**

Ontwikkeling, Hilversum

Architect **Jo Crepain, Antwerp**

Engineers **Ingenieursbureau van**

Rossum, Almere

Built in 1896, the white-plastered Villa Hoogerheide is sometimes referred to as one of the sins of Berlage's youth. Indeed, the villa is untypical for Berlage, a fairytale castle, complete with bell tower and stepped gable, with great appeal to the imagination. Sin or not, the building occupies a prominent position in Hilversum, at the highest point of the town. To make it suitable as office space, the volume was doubled with an underground extension.

During renovations in the 1980s, the former TROS broadcasting villa was restored to its original character, including the interior, complete with open hearths and panelling. Back then, the cellar was used as a bowling alley. When Johan Matser Project Development moved into the villa in the late 1990s, the usable surface had to be doubled. If executed above ground, such an extension would have destroyed the

Villa Hoogerheide

Patio and garden

look of Berlage's villa. Zoning bylaws would never have permitted such a project anyway, so a creative solution was called for. Antwerp architect Jo Crepain responded by creating the necessary office space below ground level.

The subterranean extension is circular. Two office wings with central corridors at right angles form a cross, dividing the circle into four quadrants. One of the quadrants is occupied by the villa itself. Its cellar, now outfitted as a kitchen diner, is connected to the new construction underground. The other three quadrants are sunken patios housing the offices, which are therefore supplied with full daylight. Decorated with rocks and lavender, the patios are part of the garden landscaping.

Accessed via the villa, the underground office complex does not have its own entrance. From the reception area, a broad staircase leads to a spacious central corridor laid out along the main axis. A strikingly coloured, semicircular wall – a major orientation point on the main axis – conceals the copying machine. This axis terminates at an earth-retaining wall, against which two staircases serve as escape routes.

Jo Crepain used high-quality materials. The black stone floor, walls of maple alternating with engraved glass, and the occasional colour accent create a warm, businesslike atmosphere, a contemporary contrast to the interior of the villa. With relatively minimal resources, a remarkable amount of daylight descends into the offices. Matt glass walls and a series of dome-shaped skylights supply the central corridor with tempered daylight. In the evening, the situation is reversed, with the roof lights illuminating the main route through the garden with artificial light, acting as beacons to lead visitors from the car park to the villa.

In the new construction, a system was employed that is new to the Netherlands: Triotherm. This system simultaneously regulates floor heating, cooling, heat recovery and ventilation. Fresh air is blown in via floor grids and stale air extracted via the walls. All pipes have been concealed in the floors and walls. Suspended ceilings were not used, permitting a less deep excavation pit.

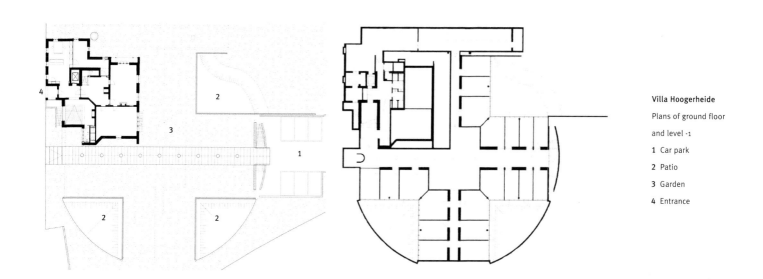

Villa Hoogerheide

Plans of ground floor
and level -1

1 Car park
2 Patio
3 Garden
4 Entrance

TWO WITHDRAWAL ROOMS

SOUTERRAIN

Amsterdam Architectenbureau von Meijenfeldt

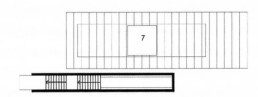

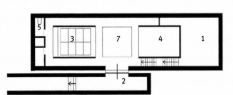

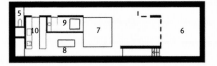

Glass Temple
Ground floor plan
Level -1 plan
Level -2 plan
1 Atrium
2 Entrance
3 Guest accommodation
4 Office
5 Lavatory
6 Exhibition space
7 Courtyard
8 Dining room
9 Bathroom
10 Kitchen

GLASS TEMPLE

Function **media room, exhibition hall,**

guest accommodation

Address **Kyoto, Japan**

Construction volume **750 m³**

Floor surface **250 m²**

Depth **6 metres**

Number of levels underground **2**

Design **1998**

Construction **1998**

Architects **Takashi Yamaguchi**

& Associates, Osaka

The idea of descending into the ground to meditate and reflect conjures associations with serene, introverted spaces. A visit to the Glass Temple is a divine experience. So supernatural is the fall of light, there is no longer any sense of being below or above ground. Awareness of the external environment is erased, it is without context – the perfect atmosphere for contemplation. You need not visit a Japanese temple complex, however, to practice such introversion: using appropriate light sources, colours and materials, a basement in an Amsterdam house was transformed into a place of contemplation.

Glass Temple

The Reigenko-ji temple complex, built in 1638 by Emperor Gomizuno-o, was extended in 1998 with a meditation room-cum-exhibition hall and guest accommodation. Architect Yamaguchi wanted to 'continue' history with a modern extension using a contemporary form language, in keeping with the Japanese tradition. To maintain the integrity of the historic building, the new temple was placed underground, if not rendered entirely invisible. Its roof, a rectangular, glass volume, protrudes subtly 75 centimetres above ground level into the Zen garden.

A central courtyard, 6 by 22 metres and 6 metres deep, was cut out of the underground construction area. Because of the translucent walls surrounding the patio, the courtyard is experienced as an interior, not as an outside space, a volume formed by a framework of matt glass. In contrast to the light illuminating the rooms beneath the glass roof, the light entering from the courtyard is soft, cool, of a slightly mysterious nature and continually subject to changes in intensity. A glance at the roof shows that we are looking along the roots of the maples, up to their very crowns. Above, only the heavens are visible, perhaps adorned by cloud patterns, and precisely this view of infinity erases all reference to ground level.

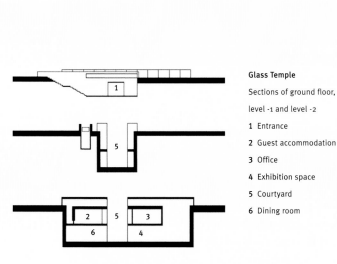

Glass Temple

Sections of ground floor, level -1 and level -2

1 Entrance
2 Guest accommodation
3 Office
4 Exhibition space
5 Courtyard
6 Dining room

Souterrain

In a basement room in Amsterdam's Old South district, designed for the lady of the house to retire from both hectic work routine and family life, this same combination of security and abstracting infinity has also proved effective.

The sense of infinity involved in this design lies not so much in its height – the room is only 2.10 metres high – but in its length, emphasised by the design of both ends. A wall of glass bricks forms a separation froms a bicycle store. A profusion of strip lighting behind the wall suggests light emanating from a clear, distant source. The other end wall is full of hollows of varying depths, and houses books, art objects, TV equipment and a computer workstation. The deep orange colours and clear lighting in the niches intensify the effects of depth.

128

SOUTERRAIN

Function house

Address Amsterdam, the Netherlands

Construction volume 230 m³

Floor surface 120 m²

Depth 2 metres

Number of levels underground 1

Design 1999

Construction 2001

Architects Architectenbureau von Meijenfeldt, Amsterdam

Souterrain

1 Main entrance

2 Garden entrance

3 Bicycle store

4 Wine cellar

Tent versus cave

Interview with Norman Foster

Samuel Beckett Theatre
Oxford, Great Britain

Whether an office block, an airport, a railway station or a metro, or structures of more modest proportions, such as a piece of furniture, a doorknob or a tap, Norman Foster works each project out in detail, convinced that the quality of the objects surrounding us directly influences the quality of our lives. Using space below ground level in order to keep life in the cities pleasant is no mere detail to Foster. On the other hand, with the Commerzbank building in Frankfurt am Main, for example, the celebrated British architect demonstrated that he has no fear of heights. Foster is a great advocate of exploiting the underground as a means of saving space above ground. For designers creating unique spaces underground, in close cooperation with engineers, the direct supply of daylight and the underground pressure forces are two major design issues.

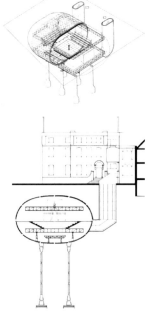

From the layout of a new airport in Hong Kong to the design of doorknobs for the Italian manufacturer, Valli & Valli, the portfolio of the British firm of Foster and Partners is very versatile. Lord Norman Foster founded his design studio in 1967. It employs some 500 personnel in London, Berlin and Hong Kong, and has carried off more than 165 prizes. Foster appears not to shrink from anything; his scope is broad. When approaching architectonic problems, he discusses the issues thoroughly with the client and all those involved, in order to produce a building with optimal working or living conditions, one that, moreover, harmonises with its urban or rural environment. In 1999, this 'philosophy of integration' earned him the Pritzker architecture prize. The jury praised him as an architect who cares passionately about the future of this planet, an avowed optimist with a firm belief in technological progress, but who also believes that architecture is about people and the quality of life.

Underground forms

To arrive at an ideal result, Foster likes to explore the limits of the technically possible, often with eye-catching results. Less well known, however, is the fact that already in one of his first designs, Foster crossed the boundary of the ground level. In 1964, when he formed the design studio, Team 4, with his then wife, Wendy Cheesman, Richard Rogers and Georgie Cheesman, he designed a house in England's Cornwall, which took the form of a semi-submerged glass ball. After this initial experience with the underground, and following the breakup of Team 4, came Foster's first totally underground experiment: a design for the Samuel Beckett Theatre in Oxford, a collaboration with Buckminster Fuller. The project was never realised, but it would probably have been a rather wet experience for the two architects. 'I remember that Bucky made the comparison with a submarine', tells Foster. 'Because the structure of the building had to be resistant to water, like a seaworthy vessel. The building had to stand up to the ground water and other natural underground forces. So it's no coincidence that my later underground projects also take the form of ships and submarines.'

Tent and cave

In designing the Bilbao metro, Foster once more allowed himself to be guided by the underground forces of nature. The result, incidentally, was realized to the full satisfaction of all concerned. As it happens, the investment in graffiti-resistant walls turned out to be superfluous, since the inhabitants of the Basque city were so proud of their new metro that no one wanted to spoil the stations. Foster did not mask the typical, hollowed-out forms that were created: 'When carrying out research into underground structures for this project, I discovered that many designers do everything they can to make the space look as if it's above ground. I object to that, because the underground can create an extraordinary atmosphere of almost religious intensity'.

What intrigues Foster is working with underground forces, the way they influence the forms of the spaces. The metro in Bilbao was excavated in the form of an arch, the ideal form for withstanding pressure. Foster would like to ennoble the typical underground forms: 'In my opinion, there are two extremes in architecture, namely the tent and the cave. Two spiritual spheres, which influence our senses in different ways. We shouldn't pretend they are the same. Whether on the scale of a house or a city, the greater the contrast in design between above and below ground and the more complex the spatial experience, the richer the experience of travelling through it can be.'

Daylight

However great the contrast between above and below ground, Foster feels it is important to ensure a direct connection between the two worlds. Metro passengers in Bilbao are led quickly to the stations by means of escalators and glass lifts, via arched glass entrances at street level, which take up the shape of the metro tube itself. 'It was an interesting challenge to provide an indiscernible link. The idea was to encourage visitors to descend, while ensuring a safe flow of passengers. I also wanted to make visiting the metro a pleasurable experience, where you don't lose your bearings.' But in addition to good orientation in underground spaces, as in all Foster's

Metro station

Bilbao, Spain

Exterior and interior

Foster and Partners

work the penetration of daylight plays a prominent role. 'With a relatively small proportion of overhead light', says Foster, 'you can animate large underground spaces enormously. Take the Pantheon in Rome, for example. A small gap in the ceiling of the construction gives the space a human feel.' As a second example, Foster cites his own design for Stansted Airport, near London. Stansted's large-scale terminal is partly submerged in the natural slope of the site, greatly reducing its impact on the rural surroundings of the Essex countryside. The building is, metaphorically speaking, upside down: functions normally situated on the roof, along with the luggage processing and other logistical activities, have been placed under the passengers' hall below ground level, leaving the roof free to absorb or reflect sunlight. Foster: 'Only five percent of the roof is fully transparent, but the results are enormous.' Light penetration not only provides a pleasant atmosphere, it is also more ecological, and artificial light can be kept to a minimum. Since there are fewer light bulbs emitting heat, there is no need for a cooling system – a key concern with underground spaces, where ventilation is always a tricky business.

Submerged landscape

With projects like the Bilbao metro, the reasons for using the underground are obvious. Foster, however, has also proposed underground solutions for other kinds of projects. Examples are the greenhouse in the National Botanical Gardens of Wales and the Crescent Wing, the extension to the Sainsbury Centre for Visual Arts in Norwich. 'In these projects, we manipulated the landscape,' explains Foster. 'The roof of the extension to the Sainsbury Centre is part of the landscape. Only an eyebrow protrudes above ground level. We opted for this solution out of respect for the green environment of the surrounding park. It had to be a space where you could detach yourself from the presence of the building. We wanted to spare the landscape by burying the building.'

The extension to the Sainsbury Centre is a token of respect for the original building of 1978 – now a listed monument, also designed by Foster. A considerable extension of the existing basements preserves the original visual impression. The Crescent Wing not only houses depots, as originally intented, but also provides space for temporary exhibitions, conferences, restoration workshops and a restaurant. Because the design integrates the incline of the ground, the underground extension becomes visible in a natural way. A sloping window admits daylight and offers a view of the surroundings. The greenhouse of the National Botanical Garden was also dug into the landscape. The roof, an enormous ellipse measuring 95 by 55

132

The Great Glasshouse
National Botanical Gardens
of Wales, Great Britain
Foster and Partners

Sainsbury Centre for
Visual Arts
Norwich, Great Britain
Foster Associates

metres, rises above ground level. Its simple form admits a great deal of light, creating an ideal climate for Mediterranean plants. Only the north side is not translucent.

Foster argues for more submerged buildings. 'Population growth and the advent of mega cities are increasing the pressure on sensitive areas. The underground has enormous potential for realising spatial benefits. You could say that one of the greatest challenges facing mankind is to achieve higher density while at the same time improving urban existence. In many cases, you can also create a certain amount of open space by situating facilities underground. Functions that traditionally take up much of the space at pavement level, such as office and industrial space, cafés and restaurants, can be partly incorporated underground to alleviate pressure at ground level. You can elaborate on that principle in an ambitious way when developing on a large scale, creating a new main level under the surface for specific functions.' Foster does not want to leave large-scale exploitation of the underground to engineers and interior decorators. 'All my projects are in some way a protest against the idea that buildings should only be designed by engineers and fitted out by interior designers. I strongly believe in a future in which the boundaries between various disciplines disappear. A quest for the integration of architecture and engineering can, for example, lead ultimately to the realisation of places that are very special because of their underground conditions, places that could never be confused with space in buildings above ground.'

4 FUNCTIONS

We can get more under ground

Ernst von Meijenfeldt and Dick Regenboog

Panopticon Prison Breda

Two Restaurants: Wagamama London

Restaurant Johan Graz

WE CAN GET MORE UNDER GROUND

Shedding light on hidden programmes

Ernst von Meijenfeldt and Dick Regenboog

In the Netherlands, development is proceeding on a scale unique in Europe. To compensate for a serious lack of space, urban areas are constantly being expanded. The surrounding countryside is under heavy pressure, particularly in the west of the country. Social functions, infrastructure and environmental interests compete for space, often simultaneously laying claim to the same, limited territory. The Dutch are no longer creating new polders, and as space becomes noticeably scarcer, alternative solutions that utilise space more intensively and efficiently are gaining in appeal. Hence, the answer to the question: why build underground? appears quite obvious. But where and how can subterranean construction contribute to meeting demands for space? Can we put even more under the ground?

With an average of 450 people per square kilometre, the Netherlands is one of the most densely populated countries in the world (population density is 15 times that of the United States, for example). There are, however, no real metropolises. The Randstad, the urban agglomeration of western Holland, where roughly seven million people live, is a network of medium-sized cities around a more- or- less open area. Absent is the highly compact urbanisation seen elsewhere in the world. Nor does any real natural landscape remain, apart from the wonderful skies and the sea. The Netherlands is more like a sparsely populated city than a densely populated country. By the year 2000, Amsterdam's population fell to just over 700,000 from roughly 850,000 in 1950, although the surface area of the city grew enormously during that period.

The phenomenon of urban sprawl is not typically Dutch, or even European. In 2000, more than half of the world's population lived in cities. Of the ten largest cities, six are in Asia, two in South America and two in North America. Europe does not even appear among the top ten. Elsewhere, primarily in the less developed countries, cities are growing explosively due to population growth and migration from rural areas. São Paulo had more than 22 million inhabitants in 2000, 100 times as many as in 1900, an index of the dramatic demographic shifts now taking place. Urban areas are expanding dramatically as a consequence of the population explosion, and the proliferation of slums and shanty towns can no longer be kept in check.

Such a situation will not occur in Western Europe, but the quality of life here is also seriously threatened. Connections are failing and roads are jamming, parts of the larger cities are becoming impoverished, and it is becoming hard to find a place that is quiet, dark and unspoiled.

Where?

Urbanisation in the Netherlands is caused by population growth, increasing individual requirements for space and a sharp increase in the number of households. Economic growth makes claims on space for new jobs, logistical functions and mobility. Furthermore, a thriving population is demanding more space for leisure activities. Prognoses of future claims on space are being continually exceeded due, for example, to incorrectly estimated projections of levels of prosperity.

Up to the present, demands for space have been met by expanding urban areas. New residential and industrial districts are being developed at lightning speed. All of them need to be supplied with gas, water, electricity and telecommunications. Waste – both solid and liquid – must be disposed of. Road and public transport systems have to serve far larger areas. These expansions are carried out at the expense of the countryside, even as the natural landscape is being increasingly appreciated and conserved, and used for recreation. Such an appreciation of open spaces, and of the countryside, is reflected in recent legislation which introduced the 'contour policy' for combating suburbanisation. This policy is intended to protect the spatial quality of rural areas by permitting urban growth only within strictly defined limits. Given almost unacceptable demands for space for living, working and infrastructure functions, forecast at between 100,000 and almost 200,000 hectares for the period up until 2030, the consolidation of existing urban areas must receive higher priority. Intensive use of space and compact development will be watchwords in coming years. The high-rise buildings, multifunctional use of spaces and subterranean construction implied by this approach are already manifest in the master plan for Amsterdam's South Axis. Several claims to space at the same location are being accepted simultaneously. Above the underground infrastructure, a completely new district is rising, with residential and office blocks, car parks, sports facilities and a public park, all realised without any expansion of the city. A large-scale urban programme is being ingeniously fitted into a space currently utilised only for an existing cluster of infrastructure.

Why not?

The best known applications of underground building are tunnels and cellars for transport and storage. Subterranean spaces are still rarely considered for other uses. There are several reasons for this. First of all, despite the long global history of underground building, it is still a relatively unknown phenomenon in the Netherlands. In countries such as France and the United States, the underground is used more frequently. Then there are also the relatively high costs of building underground. In large areas of the Netherlands, the soil is so soft that extra constructional investment is needed, while, because of location, users actually often expect to pay less. But this is not true everywhere. In Toronto and Montreal, the expensive shops are located in the vast subterranean shopping centres instead of at ground level. The same applies to the recessed Beurstraverse (the 'shopping gutter') in Rotterdam, which has the highest square metre prices in the city for commercial space.

Still, people often feel a certain aversion to staying below ground for long periods. Not surprisingly, transport and storage functions, for which underground construction is a generally accepted alternative, are characterised by short periods spent underground by people, if, possibly, longer ones for goods and resources. The potential of

Museonder

'De Hoge Veluwe' National

Park, the Netherlands

Van Hillo Verschaeren

Architecten

138

underground building for other functions, therefore, seems to depend on the nature of the activity involved and the length of time that must be spent there. None of the usual objections mentioned are insurmountable, and the government, designers and developers can draw practical lessons from them. Official information concerning underground building activities is available, for instance from the Centre for Underground Building in Gouda, the Netherlands. Investment costs for underground construction will diminish as technical knowledge progresses. The continually rising cost of increasingly scarce land makes all other factors relatively less important. The scarcity policy promoted by the contour policy is accelerating this process. Nevertheless, investment costs remain significantly higher than for building at ground level. This limits subterranean construction to cities and other complex environments, where the advantages are evident, resulting in added value not only in terms of space gained, but also in the form of improved functional and spatial qualities. As people become more familiar with appealing, well-designed underground projects, prejudice against the use of underground space will gradually diminish.

How?

In examining the various forms taken by underground building based on the criteria of 'location in relation to ground level' and 'contact with sunlight and views', three types can be distinguished. These are fully underground buildings, submerged buildings and earth-covered buildings, a categorisation less relevant for constructional than for spatial aspects. The exterior form is the characteristic element.

Fully underground spaces

Spaces entirely underground have little or no contact with the outside world. They can be either deep under the earth or just below the surface. Generally, only the entrance will be aboveground, unless access for people and goods is via the basement of another building. Buildings entirely underground are, in principle, completely dependent for light and air on mechanical means. The absence of natural light and views makes prolonged stays under ground less appealing. This type of construction is found mostly in infrastructure, in metro stations, for instance. But there are also other fully underground buildings where people spend relatively short periods, such as the Museonder museum in the Dutch national park 'de Hoge Veluwe', designed by the architects' firm of Van Hillo and Verschaeren.

Fully underground spaces are comparable to buildings without sunlight above ground, and there are plenty of those. People love to shop in the familiar closed boxes of Ikea, department stores and do-it-yourself shops.

Andersson Elffers Felix office
Utrecht, the Netherlands
Mecanoo architecten

Many people also work in such introverted environments. Most industrial estates, where the working population spends much of its time, are full of enclosed buildings.

Submerged spaces

Submerged spaces are those lying just under the surface of the ground. They can extend deep into the ground, but they always have direct contact with the aboveground world and with natural light. To admit daylight, the surface of the ground is perforated by patios, atriums and domes. An atrium can transport daylight to great depths, providing not only natural light, but also some external views. In any event, a view of the sky provides contact with the seasons, the weather and the time of day.

Providing buildings are well-designed, longer periods of time spent in submerged spaces are not only quite possible but even appealing, as in the case of the 'Glass Temple' in Kyoto. Even longer periods – a entire working day – are pleasant in the attractive and brightly designed office extensions of Johan Matser Project Development in Hilversum and Andersson Elffers Felix in Utrecht. Both the library and the two offices are submerged pilot projects that can be admired elsewhere in this book. The 'Forum des Halles' in Paris is another impressive example of building around atriums and patios on a large scale. In the same city, UN officials also work underground, in Unesco's submerged offices.

Earth-covered spaces

An earth-covered building is not, strictly speaking, under ground; it is constructed at ground level, with a surface laid over it. In the Netherlands, with its soft, wet soil, such ground level manipulations are extremely popular, partly due to such striking examples as Mecanoo's university library in Delft. This building type is free of the technical disadvantages of underground building, while enjoying its spatial advantages. Daylight can penetrate normally and views are usually unimpaired. The elevated ground level can be laid out as a park, landscape, or urban environment. In its master plan for the centre of Almere, OMA (Office for Metropolitan Architecture) opted for an urban layout on the elevated surface. One landscaped example is the design by the Von Meijenfeldt architectural agency for two industrial estates in the green heart of the Netherlands, where nature retains its dominant character by covering all commercial buildings with earth and grass. Large incisions, through which the offices sometimes protrude, supply daylight and views. In the majority of cases, earth-covered buildings can be constructed in the traditional manner. Only the roofing and

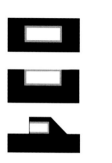

139

Typology
Fully underground spaces
Submerged spaces
Earth-covered spaces

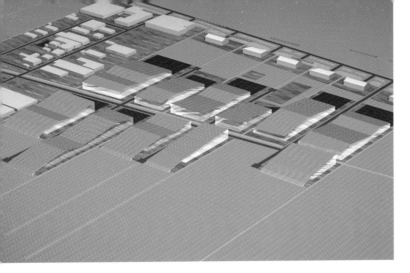

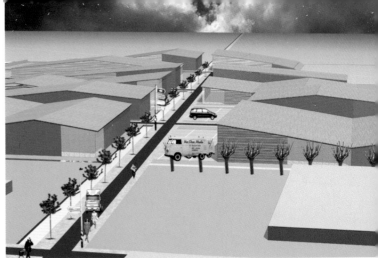

Gelkenes Industrial Estate

Liesveld, the Netherlands

Architectenbureau von

Meijenfeld

cladding of one or more facades are essentially different. In the case of noise barrier homes, a notable form of earth-covered construction, the material employed is generally sods.

In practice, all three types are found in all kinds of combined forms. Underground buildings are generally connected in one way or another with aboveground buildings. That might mean a small foyer, as in the case of the exhibition galleries for African and Asian art sited under the garden of the Smithsonian Castle in Washington DC. The museum's two entrance pavilions, designed by Shepley, Bulfinch, Richardson and Abbott, are extremely modest in size compared with the large, three storey deep, massive construction to which they provide access.

If the footprint of an aboveground building is roughly the same size as its underground parts, then these are generally referred to as its cellars. Traditionally, cellars and basements are the most accepted way of utilising underground space. Although, in the past, they were used for storing goods, these days, they accommodate many other functions. Direct links to an underground shopping centre and to the metro have made the basement of the Bijenkorf department store in Rotterdam one of the most important shopping floors.

What?

Underground functions are becoming increasingly diversified. Spaces for working, shopping, leisure time and even living are appearing alongside traditional storage and transport functions. The demands made on the space vary for each individual function, whereby the length of time spent underground plays an important role.

Living

Habitation is the most difficult function to place underground. Contact with the upper world, with light and air, is so important that rules concerning such aspects are generally specified legally. With a little ingenuity, submerged buildings are able to comply with such regulations. Underground homes are introverted by definition, and are comparable with patio homes, which appeal only to a limited group of consumers. There are more points of contact with earth-covered homes. The relationship with the outside world and the quality of life are entirely comparable with the accepted manner of house building, even where views are concerned. The noise barrier homes mentioned earlier, the subjects of experiments in the Dutch towns of Tilburg (Delmerwieden) and Utrecht (de Groene Lunet) are striking primarily due to their extraordinary sections and plans. In addition to locations with noise problems, countryside locations that are vulnerable to some degree also furnish interesting sites for earth-covered homes. The Nine Houses, discussed elsewhere in this book, were designed by Peter Vetsch to merge into the rural environment.

Certain parts of a housing programme, such as storage space, garages and sanitary rooms, can be built underground without difficulties. With reverse living, with the bedrooms downstairs, the lowest part of the residential level can be partly below grade. As with basements, windows are easy to install.

Working

Work areas can be located underground more readily than homes. That is why earth-covered and submerged companies and offices from diverse sectors, such as services, government, education, research, trade and production can be found everywhere. Their market values seem not to be adversely affected by being situated underground. After all, prices are determined by only three factors: location, location and location.

Working areas have to comply with requirements related to indoor climate, daylight, safety, health and working hours, all laid down by law. Only limited periods of work in environments without sunlight are permitted. Submerged and earth-covered working space can comply with this legislation relatively easily. The demands users make of their working environment are also subject to change. For people working on computer screens in particular – and there are more and more of them – daylight is disturbing. Those working in modern offices therefore prefer not to sit by the window, except when reading, during coffee breaks and in meetings.

The options for entirely underground working environments are limited. However, the unsightly closed boxes in industrial estates for labour intensive functions such as logistics, storage, automated production, utility facilities, transport and distribution can very well be built underground – and are sometimes better off there.

Shopping

With the success of the underground shopping mall in Rotterdam, the taboo against underground shopping in the Netherlands has been broken for good. Subterranean shopping centres have long been part of the scenery in Tokyo, Paris and Singapore, for example. It is much harder to move consumers vertically than horizontally. For underground shops, this means the need for a stronger crowd-puller to tempt consumers downward: what is referred to as goal-oriented shopping. Supermarkets, department stores, do-it-yourself shops and home furnishing shops are such attractions. Such large-scale retail trades can also be situated quite well entirely under ground. Sufficient parking facilities in the immediate vicinity are a hard and fast precondition, while daylight is not.

A combination of less compelling attractions can also succeed in enticing consumers, meaning more recreational shopping. Shops must have sufficient collective critical mass, however. Bookshops, boutiques, chemists and gift shops are not attractive enough to be situated singly underground, but in conjunction, they are. A direct connection to a metro or train station is ideal, as consumers can be drawn from passenger flows. Pedestrian flows are the driving force behind the underground shopping city in Montreal, due to its location between two metro lines. the Carroussel du Louvre, the chic underground shopping centre in Paris, a project examined in this book, also makes good use of pedestrian traffic between a metro station, the museum and a car park.

Integration of aboveground and underground shopping levels can result in sophisticated complexes, where consumers are hardly aware of where they are, a fact witnessed by the shopping units in Berlin's Friedrichstrasse and many shopping centres in the big Canadian cities, such as Montreal, Toronto and Edmonton. This also explains the success of the Kalvertoren in Amsterdam, designed by Architecten Cie. Due to the vertical organisation of the complex around a central atrium, the Hema and H&M stores have been realised in quite a natural manner underground. Visibility, safety and appeal are, naturally, important factors, but this is not specific to underground shops.

Leisure

Many people want to be entertained in their leisure time. Sports stadiums, cinemas, museums, theatres, libraries, amusement arcades and theme parks are just a few examples from the wide and varied range of activities available.

142

People enjoy visiting such buildings regularly, and spend relatively long periods of time in them. From that point of view, one might assume that leisure activities offered few opportunities for using underground space. In fact, since by their very nature many of these activities renders daylight superfluous, if not undesirable, they offer great opportunities. The long list of international underground projects proves the success of underground building in the leisure world, among them the Itakeskus swimming pool in Helsinki, the ice hockey stadium from the Winter Games in Norway, the music hall in London's Royal Academy, the IRCAM conservatory in Paris and the aquariums and nocturamas in zoos all around the world.

Daylight is undesirable for many forms of entertainment. The emergence of the experience economy, in which people are focussed on 'collecting' experiences, makes the layout of the physical space extremely important. A specific, often thematic atmosphere has to be created in the interior, for which artificial light is much more suitable than sunlight, especially when staging evocative experiences. Amusement arcades, discotheques, cinema complexes and theme parks all make good use of this tool. For these functions, all forms of underground building are, in principle, perfectly good alternatives to building aboveground, and the easy limitation of noise nuisance can be an additional advantage.

Many museums also avoid daylight. Collections are often so light sensitive that daylight is kept to a minimum in exhibition halls. The Hague municipal museum has added an underground gallery, fitted in carefully under Berlage's masterpiece, to house its renowned fashion collection.

Storage

Cellars and basements have traditionally been the storage spaces where perishable goods, wine and ice could be kept for long periods. These days, basements are used primarily for parking cars. In addition to transport, parking

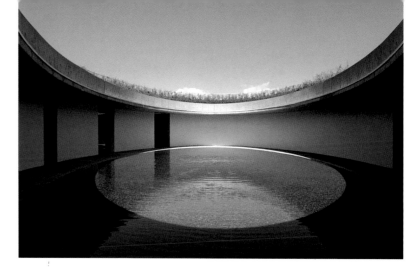

Noashima Contemporary
Art Museum
Kagawa, Japan
Tadao Ando

is the most common underground function. In the Netherlands, as a rule, new apartment complexes are provided with submerged car parks. More and more public car parks are also going underground, like those under the Vrijthof in Maastricht, the Plein in The Hague and Amsterdam's Museumplein, where coaches also disappear under ground. Public spaces are relieved of all vehicles and laid out as attractive leisure areas.

Under Post Office Square in Boston, an ugly old aboveground car park, which dominated the open space in a negative fashion, has been replaced by a well-designed underground car park. The seven underground levels accommodate more than 1,400 cars. 'Light', 'safety' and 'finish' are the key words here. The entrance looks almost like a hotel lobby, with a staffed reception and accompanying *muzak*. Ground level is laid out as an urban park. The former 'back yard for car storage', as it was commonly known, has been transformed into a green oasis. The surrounding offices are responding, by no longer turning their backs on the square, but adjusting rental prices accordingly. Now, this spot is one of the most expensive in downtown Boston.

Parking is not the only form of underground storage. All kinds of goods, hazardous substances, chemicals, waste, water, oil and gas are stored there. Here, spatial advantages and environmental and safety aspects are often more decisive than economic considerations.

Transport

Just as a healthy body depends on a well-functioning circulatory system, a well-functioning infrastructure is a matter of life or death for a modern society. The infrastructure also has its system of veins, arteries and capillaries, and there is also a major and a minor infrastructure. The minor infrastructure consists of cables and pipes for transporting information, energy and liquids, and has long been installed underground. Only when the street is dug up are we confronted with it, the exception being the odd fan who enjoys visiting the wonderful, historic sewage systems under cities like Paris, Rome and London.

The major infrastructure, consisting mostly of roads and railway lines, is far more visible. In fact, its dominance in our environment has made it a loaded subject. In general, infrastructure is seen as a burden. Radiation effects extend far beyond the actual space used, if only because utilisation in adjacent areas is limited to 'deaf' programmes (industrial estates, allotments, sports fields).

Tunnels are an obvious answer. Fully underground solutions are selected with increasing frequency and enthusiasm. In the Netherlands, tunnels are being constructed or planned on an unprecedented scale, like the high speed train link tunnel through the green heart of the country, Amsterdam's North-South metro line and

143

the planned railway tunnel through Delft. But things can always be bigger. In America, the 'Central Artery' through Boston, one of the biggest public works in the country, nears completion. The new underground traffic artery will reduce congestion above ground, improve air quality and level the barrier between the inner city and the waterfront. The heart of the city is also gaining a long public park, laid out on top of the tunnel.

In the Hoog Catharijne shopping centre in Utrecht, goods handling takes place partly underground. It is a good working example of urban supply by truck. New developments, such as unit transport by pipe, underground logistics systems and pneumatic waste transport are distribution systems that make use of underground pipes. Depending on circumstances and scale, such expensive underground systems can be competitive. It is also likely that the installation of a pipe infrastructure will mean less social resistance. Various plans are therefore being developed in the Netherlands. Cities such as Leiden and Tilburg are investigating the possibilities of underground supply for the inner city. The most advanced instance is the development of the OLS-ASH project, the underground logistics system for Aalsmeer, Schiphol and Hoofddorp. Flowers, which are time-critical goods, are transported quickly and efficiently from the flower auction in Aalsmeer to Amsterdam Schiphol airport. A connection to high-quality rail transport can also be made via a rail terminal in Hoofddorp.

When?

Underground construction is becoming more socially acceptable and even considered a necessity in some cases. Initiatives are being developed in many places. These days, in addition to the financial problems associated with higher costs, every construction project can expect objections from the community. Complaints procedures are time-consuming, and society is always wrestling with time and money. Is it really otherwise with underground

NO WAY

When the old metro line passing through Amsterdam's historic Nieuwmarkt district was constructed in the 1970s, it generated furious protest. Plans for an underground music venue near Sint-Jan cathedral in Den Bosch also led to concerns for the safety of this popular Dutch church. Now, however, building under ground is an increasingly accepted and welcome solution for unwanted development plans in the Netherlands.
The slogan 'not in my back yard' is changing to 'under my back yard, please'. Nevertheless, underground plans are not always enthusiastically received, as the websites of some major Dutch subterranean projects bear witness.

'Geen gat in de Grote Markt' (No Gap in the Town Market) is the name of an action committee set up to fight plans for an underground car park, to be combined with a large subterranean shopping square, under the market square in Groningen. Initially, the local authorities approved Jo Coenen's plan by a large majority. A referendum, however, showed that eighty percent of local residents disagreed:

'Why does everyone want to build under ground? It is a very expensive and complex alternative. This could mean the end of the Martini Towers and there is no need to build under ground.'
'When building colossal structures there is great danger of making colossal mistakes and with so much money involved, they cannot be rectified.'

'De Bovengrondse' (The Overgrounders) is an association using legal means to oppose the construction of the North-South line under the inner city of Amsterdam:
'Built on piles and built on sand is the great old city of Amsterdam / But who would pay to rebuild the town if Amsterdam should ever fall down?' asks the old Dutch rhyme.
'The North-South line is a bad choice and far too dear. It is at the expense of trams and buses, and it is unsafe, a danger to the city and an enormous nuisance.'
'Tunnel and stations fail to fulfil elementary requirements on essential points. With a diameter of 5.6 metres, the tunnel is far smaller than the Eastbound line. Many older Amsterdamers

construction? No, but there are subtle differences. More objections can be expected in historic inner cities, due to fear of damage to existing buildings and the nuisance caused by long-term, complicated construction projects. The plans for the Grote Markt in Groningen and the North-South line in Amsterdam even led to referenda. One plan foundered, while the other was granted permission, albeit by the skin of its teeth.

These are the exceptions that prove the rule. Underground construction projects that are well-prepared and thoughtfully designed, where space problems are conscientiously solved and communication has been loud and clear, are likely to evoke less resistance, as is demonstrated by virtually every example in this book.

By building whatever we can underground and whatever we must aboveground, we can compress more usable space into less surface area. The most important questions regarding the what, where and how of underground building are answered by that sentence alone. We can simply fit more underground, with less impact on the environment, less social resistance to the pollution of the landscape and less uniformity in the urban environment.

would not enter the metro for all the tea in China.'

'Local residents have dubbed the infamous subterranean project "The Hague Swimming Tunnel". The five leaks in the tram tunnel-cum-car parks have led to sceptical reactions.'

'Can't we please stop all these attempts at making the tram tunnel watertight? Let's just accept its failures and make the trams watertight.'

'Will passengers get hazard pay for travelling by tram through the tunnel?'

'Put the water back! From Prinsegracht to the Grote Markt. Like in Breda. That's what the tunnel ought to be used for. Then all that excavation won't have been for nothing!'

Concert Hall under

the Parade

Den Bosch, the Netherlands

A. Becker

PANOPTICON PRISON

Dutch Government Buildings Agency / Lex Sip

Breda

PANOPTICON PRISON

Function **prison**

Address **Nassausingel 26, Breda,**
the Netherlands

Construction volume **2,100 m³**

Floor surface **700 m²**

Depth **3 metres**

Number of levels underground **1**

Construction time **1.3 years**

Design **1997-1998**

Construction **1998-1999**

Client **Breda Penitentiary Institution,**
on behalf of the Dutch Ministry of Justice,
Custodial Institutions Department

Architects **Lex Sip, Dutch Government**
Buildings Agency, Design & Technology
Department

Engineers **DBU Industrietechniek BV, Breda/**
TES Installatietechniek Tilburg BV, Tilburg

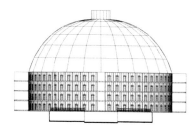

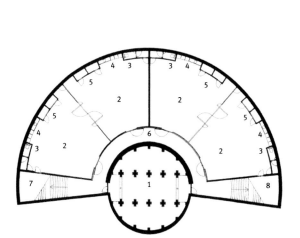

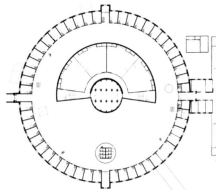

Panopticon prison

1 Gym
2 Recreation hall
3 Lavatories
4 Kitchenette
5 Telephone booths
6 Corridor
7 Broom cupboard
8 Service area

The imposing views offered by the three panopticon prisons in the Netherlands are cherished by the Dutch National Trust. Due to an acute shortage of space, the Breda panopticon was forced to expand. Although the enormous empty space of the dome could easily have accommodated the necessary keep-fit rooms and recreation halls, they would have drastically altered its original spacious design. Dutch government architect Patijn came up with a plan that would have no visible effect on the dome: an underground extension.

In 1882-1886, the architect Metzelaar built the Breda Panopticon, using the same shape and dimensions as the Pantheon in Rome. He did the same in Arnhem, and his son later used the same design in Haarlem. A functioning panopticon is even more spectacular than the Pantheon, if that is possible, because more than 200 prison inmates live between the interior and exterior walls upon which the awe-inspiring dome rests.

In 1787, the philosopher Jeremy Bentham introduced the principle of the panopticon (meaning all-seeing eye). This organisational scheme allows a large group of people to be supervised by just a few. In his model, the all-seeing eye was situated at the centre of the space, overseeing the various floors and individual cells. Solitary confinement was considered humane, for it guaranteed anonymity, enabling delinquents to begin a new lives after release. Although this principle was quickly superseded, the new building in Breda is aesthetically in accord with the panopticon concept.

In 1997, the Dutch Government Buildings Agency commissioned architect Lex Sip to design an underground extension. He had already built a shower tower from glass bricks in the dome, with which the new circular design clearly harmonises. A gym was installed in the original water reservoir under the heart of the rotunda, and a semicircle of four recreation halls built around it. For special occasions, the large doors of glass bricks can be opened and the halls combined. The transparent floor above the recreation halls extends the possibility of multidimensional surveillance. Two wide staircases lead to the core of the building.

Conditions during construction were far from ideal: all excavated soil had to be disposed of through a door measuring two metres square. Extraordinarily, work was carried out without evacuating the institution. Only when the concrete floor had to be levelled was an entire department accommodated elsewhere for two nights, by way of an evacuation exercise.

Twenty years earlier, in 1979, the Office for Metropolitan Architecture (OMA) formulated a sensational plan for extending the Arnhem panopticon underground. The unrealised plans were based on altered conceptions about imprisonment: the panopticon principle was to have been abandoned and dismantled.

To break up the centralised character of the dome, two submerged streets were to lead to the grounds outside the dome, where a conglomeration of secondary functions had been installed over time. These two streets intersected at the original all-seeing eye. Lowering its viewpoint would have deprived it of its authority. The streets were to offer access left and right to facility rooms, given some flexibility. At the same time, the submerged streets would have meant that the dome stood on a plinth, showing respect for the monument while eliminating its underlying connotation.

Arnhem Panopticon
Arnhem, the Netherlands
Office for Metropolitan Architecture

Pantheon
Rome, Italy

Panopticon prison

Recreation hall

TWO RESTAURANTS

150

RESTAURANT JOHAN

Graz Claudio Silvestrin

WAGAMAMA

Function **restaurant**

Address **10, Lexington Street, Soho,**

London, Great Britain

Construction volume **1,000 m³**

Floor surface **150 m²**

Depth **3 metres**

Number of levels underground **1**

Design **1994**

Construction **1994-1995**

Client **Wagamama**

Architect **David Chipperfield, London**

154

To a great extent, the atmosphere of an evening out is determined by the character of the establishment where it is spent. Restaurants and cafés are designed with great care, creating a certain ambience in which guests can submerge themselves. The restaurants Johan, in Graz, and Wagamama, in London's trendy Soho district, are both introverted in character. Their interiors offer totally different atmospheres, yet both are perfect down to the last details.

Wagamama

London's Wagamama restaurant is one of a chain of Japanese noodle bars. But a visit to this fast food restaurant does not mean eating unhealthy food. On the contrary, Wagamama looks after the health of its customers with a policy of balanced nutrition. According to its corporate philosophy, positive eating and positive living go hand in hand. Food is prepared in the kitchen, a showpiece situated on the ground floor by the entrance. Customers wait for tables in a long basement corridor, well-lit by floor-to-ceiling windows along the street and open roofs. Clear lighting, both artificial and natural, emphasises the purity of the restaurant's decor. The layout has been stripped of superfluous detail, including doorposts and other finishings, so stress lies first and foremost on customer and cuisine. Comfort in the old-fashioned sense of the world is conspicuous in its absence. No velvet or candlelight, just simple wooden benches at long tables, and nothing to distract diners from their meals. Here, too, the elimination of detail shows that less can sometimes be more.

155

Wagamama

Longitudinal section
and plan

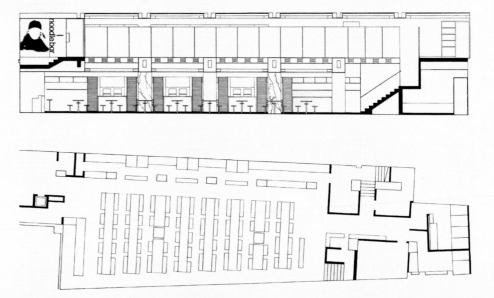

RESTAURANT JOHAN

Function **restaurant**

Address **Landhausgasse 1, Graz, Austria**

Construction volume **240 m³**

Floor surface **80 m²**

Depth **0 metres**

Number of levels underground **1**

Design **1997**

Construction **1998**

Client **Heinz Steinberger**

Architect **Claudio Silvestrin, London**

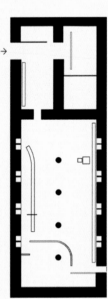

Restaurant Johan

Plan

Restaurant Johan

Wagamama's no-nonsense decor contrasts with that of the classical restaurant Johan, situated in the stables of a renaissance country villa in Graz, seat of the local government since the 16th century. In 1998, British designer Claudio Silvestrin converted the stables into a stylish restaurant. Here too, lighting plays a major role in shaping atmosphere. The impressive vaults, the original materials and the mysterious lighting create the illusion of being deep beneath the earth. The entrance, through a renaissance-era door on the street, leads into the lobby. Here, the character of the old stables is strongest. From the dimmed lights to the slate floor, everything is calculated to put visitors in the right mood. Once acclimatised, visitors descend into the crypt, where dinner is served. The narrow opening through which guests enter intensifies the dramatic effect. As at London's Wagamama, the form of the room is a simple rectangular plan, which dictates placement of tables and chairs. The kitchen is tucked out of sight behind screens.

Rooms and routes set the scene

Interview with Francine Houben

Whether motivated by lack of space or the need to retain a treasured cultural monument or natural landscape, many architects design underground buildings from necessity. But Francine Houben, founding partner of the Delft firm Mecanoo, deliberately seeks out the underground. Inspired first of all by cinema, she breaks up the relentless flatness of the Dutch landscape by elevating ground levels slightly and presenting users with ideal routings. She then presents programmes one by one, as in a script. On the other hand, her manipulation of ground level is prompted by respect for the landscape and a desire to integrate buildings, as far as possible, into their surroundings.

Houben's fascination with the landscape context translates into designs that do justice to the environment. Architects in her agency therefore work closely with urban developers and landscape architects. 'Our buildings don't cry out for attention,' says Houben. 'I think a building should be able to last 30, 50 or 100 years. In that sense, I'm aware of my responsibilities. Because if I've learned one thing, it's that programmes change continually and unpredictably. Take the villa where the management consultants Andersson Elffers Felix have their offices on Maliebaan, in Utrecht, for example, one of the loveliest streets in the Netherlands. Many villas there have been converted into offices, and when you walk along the street, you see dreary neon lighting everywhere.' When restoring the villa and constructing the underground extension in the back garden, Houben also wanted to restore its original homely atmosphere. 'A villa for working in, a sort of domestic office, seemed a good starting point,' she explains. 'The building might even become a residence again in the future, so I find expressions based purely on a programme – so rife these days – to be dubious, too easy, you might say. You are building on a foundation of quicksand, since programmes are subject to revision. Spaciousness and character are the most lasting aspects of architecture.'

Pilot in Utrecht

Mecanoo's buildings are graciously modest. Occasionally, the firm's architects seek an underground solution to integrate a building optimally into its surroundings. Meanwhile, the subterranean office extension in stately Maliebaan was necessary in order to preserve the elegant 19th-century setting. 'Rules and regulations almost prevented us from building', says Houben. 'Even underground, which is quite odd, really. I mean, why avoid building on a specific site? To retain an open space, a garden or a landscape. Even if I manage to design a project underground and keep the existing space open, it is still not allowed, because underground construction is a form of building, too. Zoning laws don't make that distinction.' In Utrecht, only an exemption granted by the local authorities and the province, once they recognised the quality of the plan, enabled Mecanoo to realise the project. 'The plan was treated as a kind of pilot that might produce encouraging results for future underground construction projects.' Which appears to have been the case: The local authorities and the province found their approach a persuasive model for future developments in the city.

Houben is pleased with the final result on Maliebaan, and she is not alone: the building was awarded the Schreuder Prize for 2001. This prize is given annually for an extraordinary performance involving the use of underground space. The jury praised the architectural perfection of Houben's design, and its inventiveness, allowing the penetration of daylight via two beautifully designed outdoor spaces. 'Glass walls look out onto these submerged patios, while window frames were placed as close as possible to the ceiling and floor for optimal light levels', explains Houben. 'The lawn behind the villa, with its centuries-old chestnut tree, was left intact, but raised slightly to create a slope, providing additional space for the underground extension. The storey height of the extension therefore rises from 2.5 metres next to the villa to 3.5 metres at the back of the garden.' The villa is connected to the new underground building by means of a lazy staircase. Two big rooms, an office and the large conference room behind it provide plenty of space. 'You're sitting here at root height, which makes the trees even more impressive.' According to Houben, the office personnel were initially scared of feeling claustrophobic. 'That's why I deliberately chose such warm materials. The walls, lit by the sun, are made from carefully cast concrete, while the other side is a 40-metre long wooden wall unit. The floors are also wood. Now, everybody thinks the room is fantastic, and it's often used for conferences. Top consultants often have guests who don't necessarily want to be seen. They can feel free in the lower space.'

Cinematic

The villa on Maliebaan fits Houben's ideal image: a house with three storeys, one of which is underground. 'When entering a building,' she explains, 'I always like being able to go either up or down. I just think it's exciting. I like to make a horizontal tour, but it's also nice to be able to move vertically or diagonally. I'm always seeking such spatial expressions, which match my cinematic way of thinking. I see designing as a way of writing a screenplay. You offer a story line, a sequence of events, like Jacques Tati does in *Mon Oncle*, for example. First this happens, then that, and then something else.' Houben feels that, with buildings, you can thus present programmes to the user sequentially, with carefully planned routing systems. 'And I really like to use the underground when designing those routes', she explains. 'Because it offers more directions to choose from. Moreover, you are far less likely to create obstructions. That is to say, if you're not careful, one part of the programme is in front of the other, and they block each other.'

159

Extension to Andersson
Elffers Felix office
Utrecht, the Netherlands

Groundwater

Architecturally, Houben finds the relentlessly flat Dutch landscape deathly boring. 'I like playing with ground level,' she says. 'But instead of digging a hole and having to dredge it, I'd rather raise the surface and create a dry underground space. This approach will become increasingly important, because, in my experience, the Netherlands is becoming wetter and wetter. For a housing complex in the Vinex district of New Terbregge, near Rotterdam, I've therefore proposed jacking up ground level a bit, so you still get underground rooms.' Car access and parking spaces there are located under an elevated wooden 'deck'. Thanks to the many atriums with their trees and the connection with this deck, the 'subterranean' street at surface level is anything but a dark, unpleasant loading zone. The elevated ground level provides residents with an extra communal outside space.

Unfortunately, Houben couldn't avoid digging one hole at Maliebaan. 'We literally had to make a swimming pool. One awkward additional factor was the absence of a loam layer under the sand, on top of which you could put in sheetpiling to pump the area out. Before we could get rid of the water, we had to pour in hydraulic concrete and make a watertight connection to the cellar of the villa. A technically complicated job.'

Dutch Open Air Museum

With the extension of the Dutch Open Air Museum in Arnhem, Houben had no problem with groundwater. The site for an entrance pavilion, exhibition space and multimedia theatre was 36 metres above sea level, which meant that routing could be partly solved underground without any problems. An obvious solution, in Houben's opinion: 'It was all about handling the crowds; we had to make a route where visitors could see everything without getting in each other's way. What's more, we had to allow for a collection of chiefly antique clothing, which can't tolerate

160

Housing complex

Nieuw Terbregge

Rotterdam, the Netherlands

any daylight whatsoever. Altogether, that made the underground the logical choice. It also provided us with an opportunity to give the theatre a dramatic form. It was a building without doors or windows, sitting like a big, mysterious egg in front of the entrance, and only accessible underground from the entrance building. For visitors, that's far more impressive than a more direct entrance.'

Library

Houben also manipulated the ground level when designing a library for Delft's Technical University. The library was raised slightly and book storage inserted underneath. Above, a sloping plain of grass serves as a roof for the ground level and first floor. An enormous concrete cone thrusts upward through all three storeys, providing, along with the glass sidewalls, light penetration. Why did Houben opt for this unique solution? 'My first problem with this design was to decide what on earth to put behind that concrete frog, Van den Broek & Bakema's auditorium', explains Houben. 'A kind of instinctive reaction was: a frog needs grass. As grass, trees and flowers fit in well on a campus, I wanted to replace the concrete tiles at the site with a big grass field. It had to be built on a particular gradient; not too steep, because then the grass would disappear and it would have become too much like a building facade.' Houben broke up the grass plain with a lazy staircase leading to the entrance of the main floor. 'So actually, you have to walk over the books to get inside', explains Houben. 'A logical layout, because upper and lower functions meet at the reception desk on the main level.' And so, Houben once again achieved her ideal: two levels above and one below ground level.

Mobility aesthetics

The library of the Technical University is probably the only example of Houben's work exemplifying the total integration of building and environment. As an advocate of visually appealing landscape, Houben lectures at the same university on her special vision, which she refers to by the term 'mobility aesthetics.' 'In our profession, mobility is a taboo topic,' she begins. 'Mobility is largely identified with driving between work and home, or to a recreational area. Noone thinks of the motorway as an amenity.' What Houben misses is a visionary plan for the design and development of urban infrastructure. 'I'd rather consider the way you experience the Netherlands from a train or a car, because we live in networks and are constantly in motion. The feeling of overcrowding in the Netherlands is all about mobility, too.' Her mobility aesthetics are intended to treat train passengers and motorists to changing urban and rural panoramas. Houben is therefore against seeing infrastructure as a drain pipe. 'Although infrastructure can be placed underground at certain points', she adds, 'a tunnel or road with a wildlife overpass over it sometimes achieves nice results. And I agree with the choice for the Groene-Harttunnel, the tunnel through the green heart of the Netherlands. Whether it's the right place or not, I can't judge, but at least, after endless discussions, a statement has been made for the landscape.'

5
PERCEPTION AND COGNITION

Through a child's eyes Diederik Samwel

Itäkeskus swimming pool Helsinki

Two churches: Temppeliaukio church Helsinki

Catedral Metropolitana Brasilia

Beelden aan Zee Museum Scheveningen

THROUGH A CHILD'S EYES

Perception under ground

Diederik Samwel

Anyone designing an underground location has an opportunity to engineer all the elements involved. Light, colour, sound, form, air and even scents can be manipulated to create an entirely new underground reality. What this astonishing fact means is that designers can exercise an enormous influence on visitors, on what they see and experience. It is, therefore, advisable for every designer to ask him or herself which physical and psychological processes are at the basis of perception, for, in addition to technical know-how, knowledge of perception constitutes the foundation of subterranean design.

We take the metro, since it gets us to the town centre quickly, but also, of course, because my daughter likes it so much. The entrance itself consists of nothing more than an escalator. My daughter actually finds it a bit scary, this black hole into which we descend. Luckily, however, there is fresh air here. Patiently, she tries to make out what is written on the blue and yellow signs.

In the train, we whizz past three stops. Suddenly, it gets light in the train. Hey? What's this? A metro that emerges aboveground? My daughter finds this most suspicious: metros are supposed to stay at least ten metres underground. We get out, walk through the central hall of the shopping centre-cum-office complex and hurry into the lift. I can see from the signs that a sports hall, restaurants, cinemas and a snooker centre have been added since I was last here. So, the city now has a really multifunctional centre.

In the meantime, my daughter, all by herself, pushes the button for the 20th floor. She can just reach it standing on tiptoes. Then she stays next to the control panel; she prefers it that way. If the lift gets stuck, she can press the alarm button herself and speak into the intercom. We exit onto the immense roof of the complex. Wow! What a view! We blink for a second as our eyes adjust to bright sunlight. Together, we work

Princess Diana Memorial
Hyde Park, London,
Great Britain
Jestico + Whiles

out which way our house must lie, look at the tiny people below and even spot a yellow train rushing along in the distance. No, she's not afraid of heights. After all, *I'm* there, aren't I? And all those other people. Apart from which, the railings are high and solid enough, even if it's very windy, she judges. We enjoy the view for a bit longer, but then we really have to descend into the shopping centre. They're bound to have those blue, half-length high-heeled boots she's been dying to get.

The lift swishes down to level -4. As yet, she has no conception of negative numbers, but she does understand that we're going deep under ground. She asks one question after another. Do I have any idea how big the underground building is we're entering? And will we be able to find the exit later on?

In a few moments, she is entirely engrossed in the floor of the central hall, which is indeed worked with fascinating patterns. Deep in concentration, she hops from one white tile to the next. We mustn't walk on the black tiles; that's the game. Then the reflective, almost luminescent panels on either side of the escalator catch her eye. Why are they so shiny?

We enter a narrow passage with high walls. Here, every opportunity has been taken to conceal the ash-grey concrete, and the upper halves of the walls are painted bright red. Neon lights on the bare ceiling are due for replacement; the tubes keep flickering on and off, intensifying the ominous atmosphere. My daughter points out a rather small fire extinguisher, and wonders whether it will actually be sufficient if a fire breaks out. In an alcove further up, to her relief, she spots a green board with white letters, which shows a little man who is running quickly away. The passage opens onto a wider, higher hall with a big fountain, surrounded by a terrace. The shoe shop is here, and luckily they've got the ones she wanted in stock. While I'm paying, my daughter wonders aloud what its like to work here all day in the dark, underground, like the man in the shoe shop: 'Don't people get a bit dopey?'

Back in the central hall of the shopping centre, she resumes her hopscotch game, abandoning it just as suddenly when we reach the exit. She runs, without hesitating, towards the light.

Childlike simplicity

Admittedly, a day out with my daughter can be tiring. But most educational, too, bringing me back to the essentials. After all, how often does this father consciously look around him in the street, examining his surroundings critically, admiring or condemning facades and letting the sight of the townscape sink in? If you want to take a better look at underground buildings, then a stroll through the city in the company of a young child is very useful, especially if perception is the key issue. What exactly do people see when they are underground? Do their subterranean experiences correspond to their expectations? Are their impressions determined by prejudice? What do they notice when entering an underground building? What appeals to them and which aspects catch their eye most readily? Do people really suffer from feelings of anxiety, of being closed in, from fear of disasters? These are the questions my daughter asks, from her own point of view, at her level of development. But not only her questions are helpful. Her behaviour and her comments immediately supply me with answers.

Children are constantly trying to find out how things work. At times, they pose trivial questions, but at others young children can touch on issues an army of philosophers could not begin to resolve. With their boundless imagination and equally limitless fantasy, children often look for the solutions themselves. The results can be surprisingly enlightening, which shows what a great advantage it is to regard the world with an open mind, uninhibited by complicated knowledge or theories.

Order and judgement

On the other hand, children are relatively inexperienced. They therefore attempt to categorise new impressions into distinctive pigeonholes, a mechanism generated by the strong need to create order and logic in their immediate surroundings. Some things seem simply impossible to a child, or else undesirable, simply because he or she has never experienced them before. Children are supposed to have two parents, and deviations are only accepted under protest. But if a marriage between two men is the first wedding experienced by a child, then a homosexual marriage is the most normal thing in the world. And, of course, the opinions of people occupying positions of authority in their environment also play a role. Children are easily influenced.

What other arguments can be offered for looking at underground buildings through the eyes of a child? Children respond intuitively, have clear-cut expectations and inquisitive minds, but virtually no feeling for nuances. No 'on the one hand.... but then again on the other' considerations. When it comes to making up their minds, children tolerate no half-measures, nor are they exactly diplomatic. Their lack of experience, their high hopes, and their prejudices lead to snap judgements, which comes in handy when looking at underground buildings. After all, most adults have learned to repress their initial reactions.

In short, there are plenty of reasons for taking a stroll through an underground location with a young child. They are not afraid to call a spade a spade. They attempt to create order in their surroundings, can be incredibly enthusiastic or terribly disappointed and, above all, bombard you with innumerable questions. Like true philosophers, they are convinced of the necessity to continually ask questions, while, being children, they also expect to remain continually in a state of wonderment.

Get them young

There is also a quasi-political reason for stimulating children to take an interest in the underground world. The way things look now, future generations will be spending considerably more time there, so they had better get used to it as early as possible. It will probably take very little effort on the part of adults to encourage them. Earth-covered houses, turf huts and pit dwellings fit in naturally with children's perceptions of the world. Heroes from children's stories, fairytales and children's videos often live in the most fantastic subterranean homes. The Teletubbies, the Wombles and the Hobbits all live in hilly underground Arcadias. And Alice falls into a rabbit hole, ending up in an subterranean wonderland. 'A home under the ground is rough and simple. It consists of one large room, as all houses should do', according to J.M. Barrie, the author of Peter Pan.

Museum of Fine Arts
Brussels, Belgium

The children's playground built in Hyde Park in memory of Princes Diana is entirely inspired by the adventures of Peter Pan. A small, earth-covered toilet block adorns the playground. The fairytale pavilion, designed by the architects Jestico + Whiles, is out of bounds for grown-ups. It is a real children's world where they can get together safely and undisturbed.

Initial reactions

What did my daughter notice during our search for the right blue shoes? Precisely those characteristics of underground buildings that make them so fascinating, although their negative aspects did not go unnoticed. My daughter's initial reactions were, in short, excitement, lust for adventure, fear, the search for shelter, the need to spot reference points, and amazement at the low penetration of daylight. In her perception, the details – colours, passageways, wall decorations, ceilings and floors – were of secondary importance.

Initially, going underground may have been a little scary for my daughter, but above all quite thrilling. Being 15 metres below surface level. without even realising it, is an adventure in itself. Still, once the initial surprise passes, the need for safety soon becomes apparent: is there a secure place to go if something goes wrong? Points of reference soon become important, but not only for emergencies; she just wants to know where she is. Usually, aboveground, you have the sun, a familiar street. a bridge or an unusual tower as landmarks. She hopes she can rely on her father to understand the directional signposting properly, and she immediately draws my attention to the yellow and blue signs on the walls and ceilings. She misses familiar points of reference. After all, these are clear landmarks for finding your way back. A more serious complaint is that there is nowhere she can see to the outside. She also seems sensitive to the use of colour and light. Why does one area feel so much nicer than another? Judging by my daughter's reactions, it depends primarily on warm colours and subdued light levels.

Research

My daughter's observations, opinions and – in some cases – merciless judgements illustrate the major characteristics of underground buildings. As it happens, anyone else can perceive them too; the intervention of an inquisitive daughter is not mandatory. These characteristics help us establish the pros and cons of being underground. What do visitors think of such spaces? Which are the problematical aspects for them? Which other aspects are perceived as positive?

Recent years have seen many attempts to answer these crucial questions, to gain a clearer picture of what exactly people notice, experience, find and expect in underground locations. Researchers have often turned to such disciplines as psychology, biology, physics or medicine. On the whole, the result has been a mountain of information about spending time underground. With this sizeable literature as a point of departure, designers can begin formulating principles for underground architecture. Which aspects, issues and principles should be taken into consideration in future designs?

Invisible

Before discussing principles, let us turn to the major features shared by underground buildings. Roughly speaking, there are three: the main shape of the building is not visible; there are no exterior facades, and therefore no windows; and – it goes without saying – users spend a certain amount of time underground. These features, perceived by visitors or prospective visitors, cause insurmountable problems if ignored in design.

Since people lack a total image of the building, they must make extra effort to get their bearings. Where is the exit? How far back does the building extend? This search for orientation and form can provoke anxiety. The submerged library in Ann Arbor (see pp. 256) does not have that problem. Skylights perforate the surface level, allowing the building's dimensions to be judged from without. In the underground extension of the Brussels Museum of Fine Arts. a central patio in the courtyard of the 'Palais des Beaux Arts' reveals the scale of the virtually entirely concealed building. Earth-covered buildings also offer exterior points of reference. From the outside, virtually nothing can be seen of the museum 'Beelden aan Zee', which is buried in a dune. But the dimensions of the dune into which the building has been fitted are visible, and this gives a good impression of its size and shape.

Associations

The second characteristic – the lack of a view – can provoke feelings of anxiety. Due to the shortage of visual stimuli and the lack of contact with the outside world, visitors may feel closed in. The number of people actually suffering from claustrophobia is, incidentally, very small. The absence of sunlight can also elicit additional fears of emergency situations. Moreover, people tend, consciously or subconsciously, to perceive a connection between windows and fresh air. They assume that a building without windows is badly ventilated. Even if the building has an extremely reliable ventilation system, it is suggestions and perceptions that count.

Comparable negative associations can also be generated by the third characteristic, the fact of being underground. Research shows that many people assume that air quality is poor and that such places are cold, dark and damp. In the worst case scenario, this increases fears of a collapse, and even of death, at least in the less optimistically minded.

An interesting question is: where do such negative associations come from? There are several answers. They may be based on previous experiences; they can be culturally determined, connected with language and language use, or even traceable back to the subconscious. It is a clever designer who tackles such general problems with negative associations at their roots. Luckily, there are also positive reactions to underground buildings. Being below ground can evoke feelings of romanticism, security, safety and protection. Nuclear shelters are under the ground for a good reason. Other pleasant associations are adventure, environmental awareness, peace and quiet and mystery. The thermal complex dug into a hill in Vals, Switzerland, designed by Peter Zumthor, is a place where body and mind can relax. The spa follows ancient Roman and Moorish customs of building subterranean bathhouses. Zumthor's work reflects almost all the aforementioned positive associations.

Psychological processes

How can negative prejudices, expectations and views be eliminated? At first sight, it is an impossible task, even if such notions were due simply to individual differences of perception. It is helpful to identify the psychological processes at the base of such perceptions, because such processes can, indeed, be influenced. Designers would be well advised to gear their architecture. for better or worse, to the physiological and psychological processes of future users.

Often, people who are just about to enter underground spaces have no idea what to expect, and that causes increased feelings of arousal (alertness). Arousal is 'emotionally neutral'. A high degree of arousal does not, therefore, necessarily imply either good or bad feelings. Environmental factors, such as complexity, colour, organisation, convenience and proportion influence arousal just as expectations do. With negative expectations and associations, such as those generated by entirely underground spaces, high levels of arousal are more likely to evoke unpleasant rather than pleasant moods. Designers can compensate by, for example, designing entrances with naturally 'arousal-reducing' effects. But designers can also exploit increased alertness to create striking, impressive environments. An underground space then quickly becomes a place of fantasy instead of merely pleasant. The virtues of the underground works of I.M. Pei, such as his contributions to the Louvre and the extension of the National Gallery in Washington DC, have been extolled by many.

Thermal baths

Vals, Switzerland

Peter Zumthor

Children, in their need for clarity, tend to classify new information on the basis of what little knowledge and experience they possess. Many adults respond to the unfamiliar – here meaning underground locations – similarly. The very same – dare I say conservative – mechanism is responsible for categorising impressions. Here, we use what are referred to as *schemata*, mental images, stored as collections of characteristics and associations, that are then ascribed to specific objects. As soon as something is perceived, it is classified into a category of objects sharing the same, or similar, characteristics.

The workings of schemata are clarified by, for example, gestalt theory, which harks back to the natural human inclination to see systematic structures, patterns and configurations where they do not necessarily exist. It is no wonder designers from the 'Bauhaus' period and painters such as Kandinsky were inspired by this phenomenon. Gestalt laws distinguish seven basic mechanisms that help to interpret forms. The laws of proximity, closure, symmetry, good continuation and similarity can be employed by designers to influence environments. Ceilings, walls and floors can be laid out according to these laws to produce, at a glance, distinct, restless, or even unbalanced images, raising or lowering arousal levels.

Strong views

Generalisation based on perception and experience is a tool for efficiently processing and categorising the enormous quantity of external information constantly confronting us. The trick is to classify the chaotic world outside into clearly defined categories. This habit is evident in widespread impressions of underground buildings. Most people have precious little experience with subterranean places, although they usually hold strong views on the subject, and not necessarily favourable ones. Underground buildings are unsafe, you easily lose your way and rapidly come to feel closed in. General expectations and schemata play an even stronger role with underground buildings, because the relevant schema – the generalised image of the underground building – is based, for most people, on a rather small store of experiences and impressions. By the same token, such expectations can therefore be easily influenced. The combined effects of the Museumplein in Amsterdam, the Beurstraverse in Rotterdam and the Beelden aan Zee Museum in The Hague are profound. Just as with acupuncture, stimulating a few well-chosen points is sufficient to cure negativity. But the reverse applies to an equal degree. Any new tunnel accident brands the entire category of underground constructions as firetraps at one fell swoop. A comparable accident in an aboveground building – a fire in a hotel, for example – is also treated seriously, but never leads to doubts about fire safety in general.

In addition to schemata, expectations and associations, attitude also plays a role in forming images of underground buildings. An attitude is the sum of an individual's ideas, feelings and opinions. Typically, attitudes are not easily influenced. Personal experiences with subterranean places, naturally, offer the greatest chance of changing attitudes. Influencing attitudes via other people or the media is less direct and effective. In view of the central position of the media in knowledge distribution and image formation, however, it is advisable to develop media plans for influencing attitudes. This can be done by supplying objective information (underground buildings are not dark, dank or scary). At the same time, subjective experiences by third parties in the form of reports or articles, for example, can provide even more positive images.

Cognitive dissonance

In theory, it goes against our nature to enter an underground construction that is perceived as potentially unpleasant. Here, another psychological phenomenon comes into play, that of *cognitive dissonance*. According to the accepted definition, cognitive dissonance is an inconsistency between behaviour and views that cannot be attributed to external factors. Loosely put: behaviour and views are out of harmony. Consequently, individuals with cognitive dissonance tend to adapt either their views or their behaviour, in order to bring the two back into harmony.

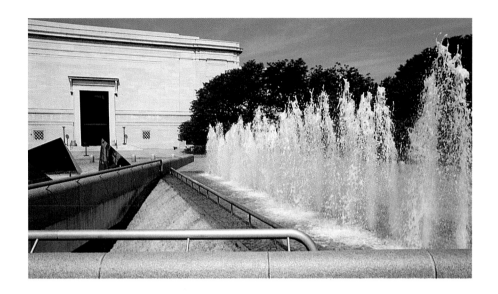

National Gallery

Washington, D.C., USA

Ieoh Ming Pei

People entering underground buildings tend to adapt previous negative views, i.e. they restore harmony by altering their views. Once inside, it is not as bad as expected, not as oppressive, chilly or dark as had been imagined. However, the process is liable to work the other way so that not the view, but behaviour is adapted. You see? It *is* dark and musty in here. I'm leaving.

Designers can take advantage of this theory. The safest course is to try to avoid all forms of dissonance, starting at the entrance, which should prevent the confirmation of any prejudices. Once inside, there may be unexpected things underground, like terraces, through-views, vistas or video images of the 'overworld', so that people may modify their judgements accordingly. Broader acceptance of underground spaces will allow a wider range of concepts and options for the designers. In the long term, therefore, the encounter with any new underground building might raise great expectations: 'These days, you should be prepared for anything when entering an underground space.' On the other hand, conscious perception of design elements causing cognitive dissonances does not necessarily lead to negative effects – but in any case there is a certain hazard. A designer opting for a dark, narrow entrance, or large spans with slim columns, runs the risk that people will adapt their behaviour rather than their views – and do an about-face.

What can be done about negative expectations or schemata? A simple answer: compensate for them with emphatically positive impressions. Make spaces light, spacious, fresh and surveyable. Because providing positive information about underground buildings is the best way to adjust images. And that can actually only happen when people spend time underground, accumulating favourable experiences. Could Stalin have known that? The metro stations beneath Moscow are palaces. It is a joy to ride the metro there, deep under ground. For Western Europeans, incidentally, this experience leads to yet another dissonance: incomprehension at so much money being spent on the metro while people were suffering in the streets.

Light

Practical research has shown that most people consider lack of daylight to be the greatest shortcoming of underground building. When making a comparison with aboveground buildings, however, it becomes clear that this is not the real reason. In offices, people often make do with far less light than they actually need, although there are far fewer complaints there about limited daylight. The real problem with being underground is the lack of views of a dynamic environment. People need to see movement and activity in the outside world.

The need for moving images and dynamics can be met by playing with views through to other spaces, or with underground courtyards with plants, flowers and people strolling around. An 'inlook' rather than an outlook. Projections of life-sized TV and video images of aboveground activities can also be useful.

Additionally, people subconsciously seek information concerning the time of day, the seasons and the weather, reflecting a natural need for contact with the outside world. People who spend long periods of time underground have problems with their biological clock becoming disorganised.

Nowadays, the necessary technology is available to limit the light problem underground to a great extent. Light has very different functions in underground spaces. People have to be able to do their work, the space must be shown to advantage, and a certain atmosphere has to be created. Furthermore, safety is an issue, and people also have to be able to get their bearings. The most obvious solution is to lower the surrounding ground level to create outdoor spaces underground. Here, daylight enters from the sides. If a high intensity of light can be achieved, then an underground space can acquire an aboveground dimension. With light wells and glass-roofed atriums, daylight enters from above. That has advantages: the light yield from roof lighting is far greater in relative terms, and light distribution is more even. There are also various ways to transport natural light deep under the ground with reflectors, such as mirrors, heliostats and other light distribution systems. In the Civil & Mineral Engineering Building discussed in chapter 4, light shafts and a heliostat transport daylight 35 metres under the ground.

UNDEREXPOSED

172

Is it really too dark to live underground? People who ask this question often fail to realise that light intensity in aboveground buildings is usually so low that their occupants live in darkness there anyway, at least in perceptual terms. In the average office, light levels range only from 500 to 750 lux, while on a spring day, outside levels reach an intensity of 10,000 lux only an hour after sunrise. To give you an idea of these levels, a candle flame at a distance of 1 metre produces 1 lux.

Light stimulates the pineal gland in the brain to carry out various chemical processes. The substances produced there regulate the biological clock. One of them is the hormone melatonine, produced in the evenings to induce sleepiness. Insufficient exposure to light disturbs the production of melatonine. Those suffering from winter depression, for example, already produce the chemical in large quantities during the day, causing a tendency to withdraw into the dark, to hibernate, as it were.

Melatonine inhibits the transfer of sensual stimuli, reducing sensitivity. In other words, light works as a stimulant, like caffeine. It increases alertness and improves performance.

Recent experiments have shown that light absorption can affect the biological clock not only via the eyes, but also, for example, via the backs of the knees.

Decreased contact with higher light intensities causes decelerated, briefer periods of melatonine production. This means the body recovers less quickly. Research shows that life expectancy for people who work at night is five years shorter than for people who sleep at night.

To avoid these effects, it is important to be exposed to light levels of 2,500 lux or higher for a couple of hours a day. Strangely enough, it makes no difference to your well-being whether you are exposed to natural or artificial light. Only the intensity of the light seems to matter.

In many cases, artificial light can compensate perfectly well for a lack of natural light. These days, daylight can be reproduced skilfully and can even imitate the times of day. But designers need not simulate; they can also dramatise, using stage lighting techniques. Finding the right light source is crucial, and so is finding the right applications for different techniques. The art is to determine the desired quantity of illumination, colour and spatial distribution. The colour and intensity of the illuminating screens of glass building blocks used by Helmut Jahn in the underground station under O'Hare Airport in Chicago make it a pleasant place to be. Strangely enough, however, the effect in the imposing metro stations in Washington DC is also very pleasant, although the level of lighting is so low as to resemble a continuous twilight. One might suppose that the stations, based on subtle variations of the same powerful design by Harry Weese Associates, would be socially unsafe, due to the lack of colour, light and stimuli, such as advertisements, but that is far from the case.

Flows and points

What else do designers need to consider? Dealing with pedestrians in public corridors, squares and inter-sections in an underground complex is an entirely different story. In a certain sense, designers can treat this underground traffic like the flows of liquids and gasses. By analogy with accepted theories from hydrodynam-ics, nodes and antinodes can be distinguished within a flow of people. At these places, the flow of pedestrian traffic is either faster or slower. Equally, the smoothness of the walls – whether the surface of a waste pipe or the wall of an underground corridor – also determines the rapidity of flows. Since moving from one place

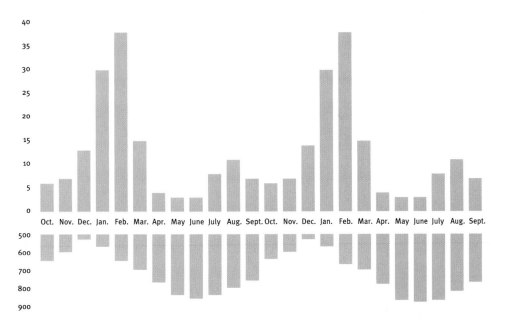

Daylight perception

The effect of daylight on people's moods.

Above: number of people who feel worse, given in hundreds

Below: average daily period of light in minutes

Subway station
Washington, D.C., USA

to another through a corridor costs pedestrians time, they tend to choose the shortest routes. These can be indicated by simple floor patterns. Hurrying pedestrians will follow the most direct route, either consciously or subconsciously. But to prevent everyone from taking the inside corner, the trick is to make the outside corner more appealing, using wall decorations, posters or, in shopping centres, placing display racks at these points, for example.

Ceiling height is also an important design element. Often, the philosophy is: the higher the better, but that is not always true. Where people wish to maintain an anonymous distance. i.e. in stations, it can hardly be high enough. But where people meet and stand or sit talking, lower ceilings are definitely better.

Essentially, there is no difference between guiding an underground and an aboveground flow of pedestrians. What designers do need to take into account, however, is that people underground need to be able to move as safely and comfortably as possible. It is therefore important to ensure optimal 'legibility' of passageways. By legibility, we mean the ease with which people can form a clear image of their environment. Underground, we rely on landmarks, routes, borders, intersections or distinctive areas to get our bearings more easily. Characteristic elements of the design ought to have clear identity and significance, whereby designers can draw from a rich array of variables, opting for unusual forms, striking dimensions, depth or relief effects, varied colours or less typical materials.

Contrasts

To increase legibility, it is also a good idea to make use of contrasts in design, such as open versus closed, vegetation versus stone, high versus low, restful versus busy. It is quite possible to accentuate special places (an exit, square, a transition to another level) by using a different kind of ceiling, or a higher intensity of light, possibly strengthened by a reflective ceiling. The secret is to find the right balance between restfulness and diversity. Will the environment become too busy if we fit mirrors on the ceiling? Or do reflective ceilings add a feeling of spaciousness and safety?

Other possibilities are the use of repeating colours and materials. Designers can deploy such variables at will, making them 'readable' as symbols for a route, a sector of a building or complex, or for connections or

intersections. Easily readable names, signs or symbols are, of course, excellent tools. Columns and pillars can also be used to communicate. Where possible, clear time relationships are desirable in underground passageways, allowing pedestrians to, for example, estimate from their surroundings how far an entrance or exit is and how long it will take to reach it.

Designers of underground buildings should realise that the architecture is usually determined all at once, as opposed to a varied environment that emerges naturally over time by means of additions, extensions, renovations, rebuilding or redevelopment. This can constitute a problem, because designers are generally geared to deciding on one building plan, not to creating several plans simultaneously. With larger complexes it can be useful to enlist several designers with different styles. A supervisor can evaluate the various plans, as is increasingly the case with large aboveground housing or utility projects. In this way, a cohesive series of underground spaces is created, each evoking an individual atmosphere, so that the transitions between spaces can acquire striking forms and appearances of their own. It is, however, essential that a corridor linking two larger spaces should bear the characteristics of both spaces. This makes for smooth and clearly 'legible' transitions. In this way, the total underground construction ultimately becomes a varied, interesting and exciting environment. The various shopping units in Berlin's Friedrichstrasse, which are linked underground, exemplify such a varied total image.

Visual stimuli

For some users, an exciting, adventurous design immediately compensates for a lack of visual stimuli. This is particularly true for those who miss the dynamics of the aboveground world and have too low a degree of arousal, which can lead to boredom and ultimately to negative perceptions of underground space. To ensure that people down below remain alert, the environment needs to be stimulating. Strategies for meeting this requirement will depend largely on the length of time spent underground and the types of activity being performed there. Someone working in an underground shop and executing relatively simple tasks needs more environmental stimuli, while someone carrying out a complex, responsible task for shorter periods probably has no time or concentration to spare for noticing the environment.

Taganskaya metro station
Moscow, Russia

Sokol metro station
Moscow, Russia

175

United Airlines Terminal 1,
O'Hare Airport
Chicago, USA
Murphy & Jahn

Of special importance is ensuring that transitions from above to below take place as gradually as possible. This is essential for adequately preparing visitors for their temporary stay underground. Here too, however, designers have some room to manoeuvre. In some cases, even conveying a conflicting impression can be successful, as at O'Hare Airport in Chicago, where passengers disappear almost literally into a black hole via a steep escalator, only to reemerge in a fantastically lit, spacious passageway full of visual stimuli.

In that case, the effect of surprise cancels any negative expectations or associations. On the other hand, the entrance is generally the only part of an underground building visible from above. There is therefore much to be said for making the entrance an attractive, tempting frontispiece. Also, it is undesirable to create too great a difference between above and below ground designs. The greater the contrast, the more likely visitors will become aware of being in a different kind of space. For the same reason, it is important to opt for recognisable, architectonic styles and interior designs.

Fear

How can fear of underground locations be combated? The relative absence of stimuli underground can lead to people feeling ill at ease, so active stimulation is important in subterranean spaces, whether using light sources, atriums, mirrors or reflectors. The presence of other people – either stationary or moving – is also important. Furthermore, people feel far more comfortable in an underground space if there is a clear plan for emergencies. Escape facilities must be clearly indicated. The same applies to signposting.

The fact that directional signposting requires precision can be seen clearly at Lisbon airport, a medium-sized facility, where twenty or so flights arrive and depart every hour. The halls and corridors rarely offer views of the outside world, but are, in general, spacious and high, which is pleasant. But there are also narrow, low passageways and narrow staircases where queues often form, causing delays during peak hours. Then spaciousness gives way to an oppressive feeling. People unused to flying and anxiously trying to find their way may well find these spots disturbing. The yellow signs for the most important messages are clear, as is usually the case in airports and other busy pedestrian areas. After all, yellow, the most striking colour, attracts attention. More ambiguous, however, are the arrows on the yellow signs. They point upwards where pedestrians are to continue straight on, but an escalator is often in sight. Should the passenger continue, or take the escalator? Harmonisation between signs also leaves something to be desired. At one place, you are told to turn right to go to the arrivals hall, while a sign twenty metres further along tells you to go straight on for the same destination. Many passengers, as a result, stand in the middle of the aisle studying the signs and blocking the way.

New World

Literature and research provide many more focuses, tips and advice for designers of underground buildings. It is also advisable to take a critical look at existing subterranean constructions. Apart from a thorough theoretical and practical preparation, however, it is a good idea to consider the nature of the work during the design process. What exactly is the designer doing? Essentially, he or she is creating a completely new world. Like a film director, with virtually all the elements at his or her command: light, sound, colour, form, air and odour. With so many possibilities and so much responsibility, it can refresh the mind to take a break now and again and, for example, consult a concise philosophical work. After all, philosophers are skilled at continually posing fundamental questions.

Is it really so strange to start using underground spaces? In the Stone Age, an underground shelter without natural or artificial light, decorated walls, signposting, lifts or escalators was absolutely normal. A cave was the perfect place for sheltering from danger, whether from animals or the climate.

Plato's Cave

Much later, some 24 centuries ago, the Greek philosopher, Plato, used the cave as the crucial scene to explain his theory of Ideas. Briefly summarised, his theory states that the things perceived by man are only reflections of ideas. What we perceive with our senses is nothing more than the outward manifestation of those ideas. It is not by means of our sensual perception, but by thinking that can we visualise this realm.

In his Dialogues, Plato describes the analogy of the cave. A group of people are chained up in the middle of a cave, warmed by a big fire, which is behind their backs and invisible to them. From time to time, on the wall directly opposite, appear shadows of people, animals, plants and other objects, which they name one by one. As far as the group knows, this projected shadow-world is the manifestation of reality itself. Suddenly, one member of the group succeeds in escaping. Looking for a way out, he realises that reality is different, after all. He discovers a real shadow play. Concealing themselves behind a little wall, between his chained companions and the fire, several people are holding up all kinds of objects – carved dolls, animals or plants – one after another in the light of the fire, so that their shadows are cast on the wall at the back of the cave. The escaped prisoner suddenly sees the light when he manages to reach the cave mouth, where he sees the originals of the images in the cave in real life. Dazzled and dumbfounded, he walks back to enlighten his fellow prisoners. They, however, are not going to be persuaded that easily. Who does he think he is, coming and destroying their view of the world without so much as a by your leave? Finally, emotions run so high that the messenger pays for his account with his life.

Plato's analogy will always remain relevant. Children, philosophers and also the odd innocent layman, still wrestle with the question of what they actually perceive when they see a horse standing in a meadow. Is it *a* horse, *the* horse or a member of the Equidae family? All things considered, our perceptions, founded as they are on generalisations and categorisations in accordance with the schemata and gestalt principles mentioned earlier, can be traced back to ideas.

Now that we are, once again, preparing the underworld for use, Plato's cave analogy becomes even more fascinating. Technology is not really the problem, nor is safety. Our discussion clearly shows that the biggest obstacle to the large-scale use of underground space lies with the users themselves, with their views and expectations. People feel scared, closed in and unsafe when deprived of contact with the outside world. What can we do about it? The solution is simple, but its execution immensely complicated. Designers are faced with the task of organising the environment underground just like the one above – from the basic out-lines down to the tiniest details. From light and colour to inlook and outlook. And, above all, with clear, direct connections to the aboveground world, using domes, underground courtyards, atriums and video images. Perhaps the messenger from Plato's cave would have fared better had he been able to use the latest video technology.

The evening after our visit to the underground shopping centre, I was reading my daughter a bedtime story. We were in the middle of Roald Dahl's *Fantastic Mr Fox*, a book that also gives a great deal of pleasure to adults. It is all about a bold, resourceful fox who time after time, manages to outwit three vengeful – but rather naive – farmers. Time and again, the fox manages to escape together with his entire family and, later, with their friends, the Badger, Weasel and Rabbit families, from the clutches of the farmers, who are after his blood. The farmers are determined to put an end, once and for all, to their tormentor, who murders chickens and geese and steals many other riches. While they stand watch at the entrance to his den, guns at the ready,

THE UNDERWORLD

Despite all his wanderings, Odysseus never reached this place. Orpheus, in an attempt to retrieve his beloved Euridice, did. The place is Hades, the underworld of Greek mythology.

With pitch-black fire in his eyes, Charon ferries souls across the currents of the river Styx (the 'horrifying') to the underworld. Each carries a coin under his tongue to pay the ferryman for the crossing. Then there are the souls he refuses to take across, those who have had no burial. Life here is colourless. On the far side of the river is the entrance to the kingdom of Hades, an enormous gate guarded by Cerberus, the three-headed dog with dragon's tail. His fierce bark and stinking breath ensure that no-one dares escape. Once, however, he was caught off guard by someone who threw him a cake of honey and wheat, filled with a sleeping draught.

After the gate is the neutral zone of the kingdom. Here, amidst monsters and demons, dwell the children, those who were con-demned to death as a result of false accusations, and suicides. In the valley abide souls tormented by unrequited love.

In the distance lies a parting of the ways, and in the far fields beyond this fork reside souls who won fame in battle.

The fork in the road nears. To the right, the path dips under the gigantic palace of Hades into the Elysian Fields. To the left, the way leads to Tartarus. Before one of these roads may be trodden, the dead must be judged by a tribunal. Elysium is a blissful place, with its own stars and sun. Those who dwell here exercise their various crafts in the fields or wrestle on the sands. Some dance; some sing or recite poems. Those yet to be born live here beside souls destined for reincarnation.

But not everyone returns to Earth. Some remain forever in Elysian. The less fortunate go to dismal Tartarus, lying far beneath the roots of the earth and the bottom of the sea. Yes, even deeper than the palace of Hades. All rivers flow into the abyss of Tartarus. It is a well-guarded prison with a gate of indestructible pillars, which even the gods cannot destroy. Now there is no escape, and those who enter suffer forever.

Mr Fox effortlessly finds various underground escape routes, and it is a piece of cake for him, en passant, to raid the storerooms of his enemies. Of course, Mr Fox comes out all right in the end. The book ends with a celebratory meal, the table laden with looted goodies. I close the book and switch off the light. My daughter is extremely impressed with Mr Fox. 'He's so clever. People can't do things like that, can they? The way he finds his way under the ground. And he doesn't even need a torch.'

ITÄKESKUS SWIMMING POOL

Hyvämäki-Karhunen-Parkkinen

Helsinki

ITÄKESKUS SWIMMING POOL

Function **swimming pool**

Address **Olavinlinnantie 6, Helsinki,**
Finland

Construction volume **61,000 m³**

Floor surface **10,210 m²**

Depth **32 metres**

Number of levels underground **2**

Construction time **4 years**

Design **1987-1991**

Construction **1989-1993**

Client **Municipality of Helsinki**

Architects **Hyvämäki-Karhunen-**
Parkkinen Architects, Helsinki

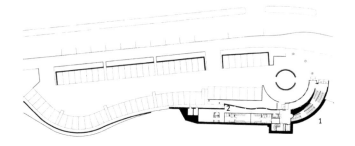

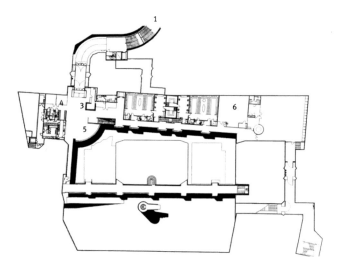

Itäkeskus swimming pool

Ground floor plan

Level -1

Section

1 Entrance

2 Personnel entrance

3 Counter

4 Lockers

5 Café

6 Gym

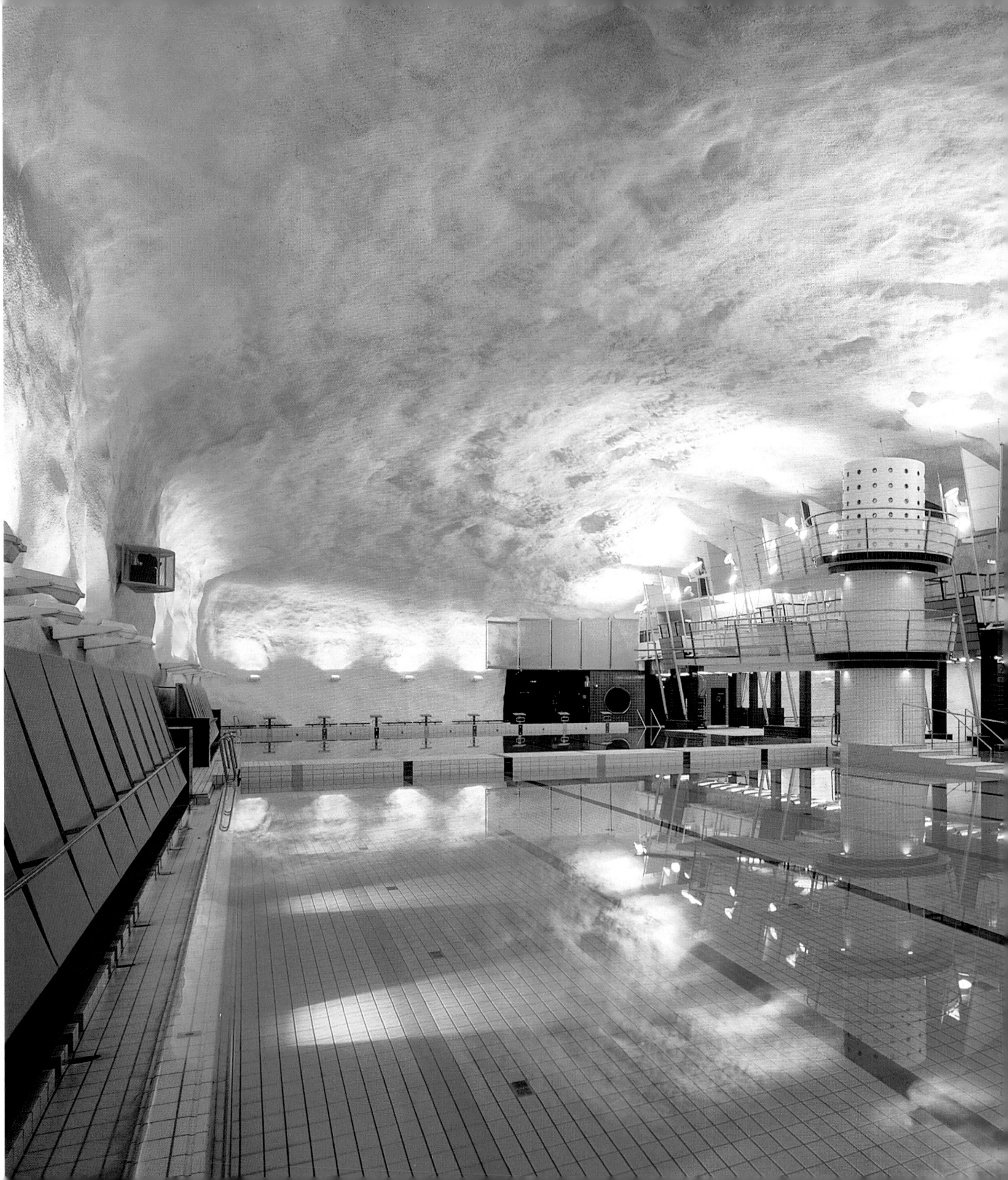

184

Finnish law obliges local governments to provide facilities in case of a nuclear attack or disaster. Since these areas are not permitted to have direct links to light or air, the obvious solution is to create underground shelters. In a central nature reserve in a suburb of Helsinki, both a swimming pool and a shelter were needed, so the two projects were combined, greatly reducing the high construction costs associated with stone cutting.

The complex is situated in a relatively easily worked rocky hill in a thickly wooded nature reserve. The underground location eliminated the need for building in the park. Only the entrance is above ground, a glass pavilion beneath a striking semicircular porch that seems to emerge from the bowels of the earth. Upon entering, visitors begin an impressive journey into the underworld via a wide flight of stairs. The route twists and turns: given the danger of multiple shock waves after a nuclear explosion, access to the shelter may not be continuous with the entrance and main area.

Your sense of direction is put to the test by the winding route. At the point where contact with the outside world ceases, the main space opens up. This level houses the cash desk, gyms and a café, and has views of both the swimming pool and the access doors to the shelter. As the corridor is not straight, visitors quickly have the impression of being deep under ground, although the reception hall is only five metres below surface level.

At the lowest level, beneath an enormous arched white roof, are the swimming pools. This is a real aquatic paradise with a fifty-metre pool, training pools, children's pool, relaxation pools, whirlpool baths and jacuzzis. The facility is completed by a complex of facilities, from saunas, Turkish baths, solaria, showers, changing rooms and conference rooms to high quality facilities for rehabilitation and physiotherapy. Under the granite vaults of this subterranean space, a ceiling has been fitted to more or less follow the contours of the excavation. This ceiling prevents condensation and creates installation space. Its surface has been made to imitate a cloudy sky. The constantly moving play of light on the ceiling, cast by the water's reflections, makes the room seem higher.

Feelings of claustrophobia and unease are reduced by variations between small and large spaces, while the clearly-lit, illusory cloudy sky denies the underground location. Still, the place where ceiling ends and walls begin is dark and mysterious, intensifying the sensation of being in a cave.

185

Itäkeskus swimming pool
Entrance

TEMPPELIAUKIO CHURCH

Helsinki Timo and Tuomo Suomalainen

TWO CHURCHES

CATEDRAL METROPOLITANA

Brasilia Oscar Niemeyer

In religious buildings, light entering from above has a powerful significance. Two subterranean churches in Brasilia and Helsinki emphasise the poles of heaven and earth. Both have been submerged into the ground and given dramatically designed light roofs. Worshippers at Oscar Niemeyer's Catedral Metropolitana in Brasilia enter through an underground corridor. Salvation and forgiveness await the human soul at the end of this dark, ritual passageway. In Helsinki, the Temppeliaukio church may be entered from street level, but a similar chastening effect is achieved by entering the beautifully lit church via openings in its thick walls, hewn from the rock.

Temppeliaukio church

The Temppeliaukio, built to designs by Timo and Tuomo Suomalainen, was hewn from rock using elementary tools, and roofed with a copper dome. A skylight running around the entire circumference forms the transition between dome and rock, so the roof appears to float. The naked rock has been left exposed and unfinished and water is allowed to seep in and trickle down the walls. Only a few small fissures caused by dynamite have been repaired, and a single large crevice has been used to create the altar. Since opening its doors in 1969, Temppeliaukio has become one of Helsinki's greatest tourist attractions. Besides use for services, the church provides a spectacular setting for congresses, symposia and concerts. During such events, the air-raid shelter under the church, built during the Cold War, is used as a car park.

Temppeliaukio church
Altar

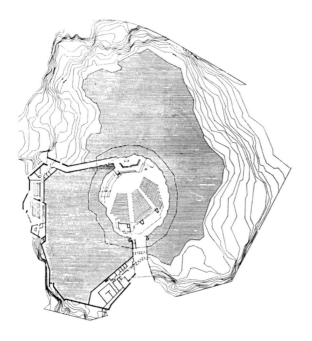

Temppeliaukio church

Site plan

190 Section

TEMPPELIAUKIO CHURCH

Function **church**

Address **Lutherinkatu 3, Helsinki, Finland**

Construction volume **6,000 m³**

Floor surface **950 m²**

Depth **6 metres**

Number of levels underground **1**

Construction time **8 years**

Design **1960-1961**

Construction **1961-1969**

Architects **Timo and Tuomo Suomalainen, Helsinki**

Catedral Metropolitana

The enormous plain alongside the Esplanada – the main axis of Brazil's capital city, and the site of the parliamentary buildings, also designed by Niemeyer – leads to the shady side of the Catedral Metropolitana. This approach enables pilgrims to prepare themselves for the religious spectacle that awaits within.

The Catedral Metropolitana is part of a complex consisting of three elements: the church, the free-standing bell-tower and the baptistery. The underground church is reached via a long, descending slope in the ground. Its dome is composed of sixteen boomerang-shaped concrete ribs, the buttresses of the church, held together from above and below by two concrete rings. Splendid blue-green stained glass between the ribs, painted by Marianne Peretti, creates a divine atmosphere. This modern church harks back to Gothic traditions, while its ideal form and symmetry give it a somewhat classical look.

CATEDRAL METROPOLITANA

Function **church**

Address **Esplanada dos Ministerios**

Brasilia, Brazil

Construction volume **6,500 m³**

Floor surface **700 m²**

Depth **4 metres**

Number of levels underground **1**

Construction time **10 years**

Design **1959**

Construction **1970**

Architect **Oscar Niemeyer, Rio de Janeiro**

Catedral Metropolitana

Interior

BEELDEN AAN ZEE MUSEUM

Wim Quist

Scheveningen

Beelden aan Zee Museum

1 Entrance

2 Coffee area

3 Counter

4 Library

5 Office

6 Exhibition area

7 Exterior exhibition area

8 Storage

9 Sea Hall

10 Wilhemina Hall

11 Workshop

12 Library

13 Entrance to study area

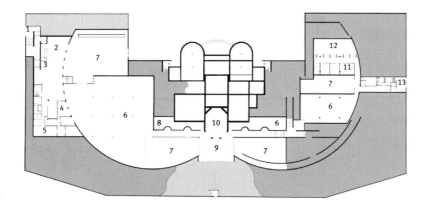

MUSEUM BEELDEN AAN ZEE

Function	**museum**
Address	**Harteveldstraat 1, Scheveningen the Netherlands**
Construction volume	**6,000 m³**
Facade surface area	**3,800 m²**
Floor surface	**1,800 m²**
Depth	**6 metres**
Number of levels underground	**1**
Construction time	**1 year**
Initiative	**1989**
Design	**1989-1993**
Construction	**1993**
Client	**Scholten-Miltenburg family**
Architect	**Wim Quist**
Engineers	**ABT Arnhem (Rob Nijsse)**

Many development plans had been proposed for the site of the neo-classical Von Wied pavilion in Scheveningen, 200 metres from the spa house. Proposals ranging from two diplomatic residences to a shopping centre all encountered fierce resistance from local residents, who wanted to retain the open space. In the end, the desire of the founders of the sculpture museum, Beelden aan Zee (or Sculptures by the Sea), to exhibit their extraordinary collection in the dunes was fulfilled with a powerful design by Wim Quist.

Nestled into a dune, the museum is entirely concealed from view. The dune itself is contained by a concrete retaining wall, its entrance an inconspicuous opening. The museological space is housed in two semicircles and embraces the De Witte pavilion, on top of the dune, with an expansive gesture. Between the semicircles lies a chain of exhibition halls. The semicircle containing the entrance is covered and flows into the second semicircle and the exterior exhibition space. Two circular walls, as smooth as stone, have been constructed from concrete cast on site, and given a sandy colour by the addition of aggregates.

    The museum's introverted atmosphere contrasts pleasantly with the hustle and bustle of the promenade. The light here, made famous by the painters of the Hague School, penetrates via skylights and glass-screened patios. This play of light and shadow on the

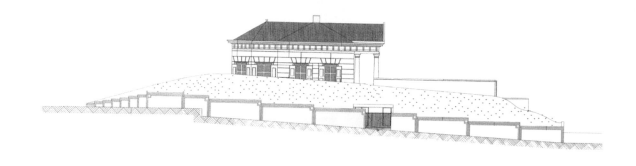

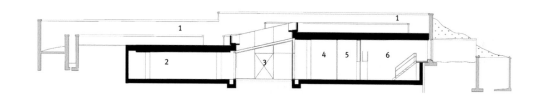

Beelden aan Zee Museum

Side elevation and

section of new building

1 Exterior exhibition area

2 Exhibition area

3 Patio

4 Workshop

5 Corridor

6 Library

199

walls suggests the presence of a row of windows. Deeper within, the museum renounces its surroundings. Halfway along the exhibition route, in the Sea Hall, where the two circular segments intersect, is a panoramic view of sea and clouds. Adjacent are the white stuccoed subterranean vaults of the pavilion. Outside, the rising terraces reveal the pavilion, the pier and the buildings on the promenade. But the surrounding area remains at a comfortable distance. Strolling visitors finds themselves on an island, far removed from the immediate vicinity.

The Delfland Dike Board stipulated that no sand was to be removed from the range of dunes during the works, since this material is the primary sea defence in the Netherlands. The board agreed to the project on the condition that the sand dug out would be used elsewhere along the coast. A considerable quantity was replaced on top of the building, which, naturally, had consequences for the construction. The roof of the entrance was covered in a 90-centimetre thick layer of concrete. In the concrete circular walls, the stainless-steel central pins and conical 'stops' form a rhythm of silver-coloured accents. These holes were deliberately left unfilled, enabling them to serve as a uniform mounting system.

Quist has drawn up a design for an additional underground extension. The idea is that the circular segment currently housing the exterior exhibition will be hollowed out to make room for extra exhibition space and a research institute for sculpture. The profile of the existing retention wall on the east side will therefore support an insert floor for the library. The new building will be given an extra entrance via a gate on the south side. As the extension will be situated under the terraces, no exhibition space will be sacrificed. One part of the 120 m² of exterior exhibition space will, however, be lowered to the level of the new building, but this patio will also function as exhibition space. It will then be possible to see the sculptures by the sea not only at eye level, but also from above.

No ostrich policy

Interview with Jan Benthem

Amsterdam's Schiphol Airport, the Zeeland Archives and Amsterdam's North-South line are all major underground construction projects that betray the hand of Benthem Crouwel Architects. It does not follow, however, that this Amsterdam firm avidly supports the use of underground space. In Jan Benthem's view, the way downward is often an escape route for local governments who dare not take responsibility for aboveground solutions. An ostrich policy, in other words. But when space shortages aboveground make the underground the only alternative, then the architect needs to be involved in the project from the concept phase onwards.

The work of Benthem Crouwel Architects is characterised by clarity, sobriety and functionalism. Much attention is devoted to functionality and logic, without getting bogged down in stereotyping. For this reason, the agency has proved an ideal partner in devising daring solutions to complex urban development and infrastructural design problems. With such assignments, the programme is often not dictated by classical factors such as the number of m^2, organisational schedules or technical requirements, but by seemingly peripheral issues, such as political decision-making, traffic flows and transfer times. The architect is generally not given a mandate in the traditional sense, but must skilfully and sometimes aggressively defend his ultimate prerogatives as designer. One precondition for a successful, aesthetically satisfying design is the forging of workable coalitions in a complex interaction between various parties, while the designer needs to retain his independence. Amsterdam Schiphol Airport is a wonderful example of this. In the 1980s, Benthem Crouwel Architects, together with the Netherlands Airport Consultants BV, developed a master plan for tripling the airport's capacity. The underground was fully included in the plans. At Schiphol Plaza, completed in 1995, various above and below ground levels have been brought together. There is public access to the shopping centre, the car parks, the WTC and the national railway station, which is deep under ground. At Schiphol, not only is underground space used for controlling passenger and visitor flows. Internal logistics and luggage and goods handling also take place partly under ground level.

The North-South line
According to Jan Benthem, Benthem Crouwel's underground experiences at Schiphol were not the immediate rationale for choosing the agency to design the aboveground and underground metro stations of Amsterdam's North-South line. 'It was more because of our knowledge of the logistics involved,' he explains. 'The technical principles for the construction of the stations were, of course, already established when we started the project'. For the low level stations – Rokin, Vijzelstraat and Ceintuurbaan – they opted for the deep wall method. Deep walls will be inserted into trenches to a depth of 40 to 50 metres and the surface built as a cover on top of these walls, before executing work below ground. The stations can then be constructed with minimal disturbance to activities at urban ground level. A different technique has been chosen for Central Station, where a caisson will be submerged into a deep pit. 'The arrival of the metro, together with the plans concerning Zuidas, prompted

the nearby RAI exhibition centre to develop extensive new plans, to be designed by us as well', says Benthem. 'The various techniques for the different stations did not, incidentally, lead to different architectural designs. The architecture of the entire line is quite uniform.

Only at Ceintuurbaan, where due to lack of space between buildings, the drilling tunnels run above rather than alongside each other, will a completely different station be created, simply because the logistics are different.' The climax will be Central Station, not only because of its spectacular design, but also because of the logistical unravelling and interweaving of trains, metros, buses and ferries, accomplished through great perseverance.

Safety

With the Jubilee Line, which links the centre of London with the Docklands, a great deal of money and care was spent on safety. 'A second access system was installed to serve as an escape route in emergencies. Of course, all of this is due to recent accidents in London's tube system. Although there is also an optimal guarantee of safety on the North-South line, the approach in London is, in comparison, perhaps more than optimal.'

The North-South line is seven kilometres long and cost 1.5 billion Euro. The Jubilee Line is five kilometres longer and has a budget of 4 billion Euro. 'For that price, you can afford spaciousness and a luxurious level of finish, which works in favour of ambience and social safety', says Benthem. And the latter is of inestimable value. 'Which is why I feel that Dutch architectural engineering firms should develop far more expertise in the area of social safety.' To increase the feeling of safety on the North-South line, Benthem Crouwel have, for example, made as many spaces as possible column-free. 'This creates views,' explains Benthem, 'and contributes to social safety, as does bringing passengers together in one space. It is all about ensuring sufficient numbers of people in the right places.' Benthem feels that situating other functions, such as shops, in the transition zone between the metro stations and the city significantly helps to create positive perceptions of underground space. 'For political reasons, that was initially not an option with the North-South line', he says. 'Gradually, however, it is becoming apparent that there is more room to make connections with the immediate environs. We are doing our best, as an agency, to alert the client to such added value. At the Ceintuurbaan station, for example, we are seeking links with the basements of large chain stores.'

Schiphol Airport
Amsterdam, the Netherlands
Train station

Schiphol Plaza

201

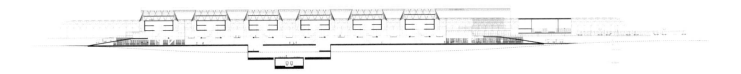

Zeeland Archives

In addition to Schiphol and Amsterdam, Benthem Crouwel also went underground in Middelburg, where the Zeeland Archives wanted to build an extension. In the garden, behind the 18th-century mansion house, there was room to dig a 13-metre pit. A thick concrete floor was cast on top of the soil, after which three depots were constructed, one on top of the other, for storing archival material, for example. 'Which,' comments Benthem, 'is actually forbidden. In principle, it is not allowed to store items of cultural heritage underground, due to the risk of flooding. In Maastricht, at the Limburg Archives, there had been long-term problems with underground water currents running just underneath the building. Despite all precautionary measures, moisture continued to seep through the walls. It provided us with extra knowledge on how things should be done. To make the space water and damp-proof before building the concrete basement, we first welded together a seamless steel excavation pit, which acted as a permanent formwork. Solutions using damp-proof foil were rejected due to its vulnerability. You only have to miss by a centimetre with a bar and you've got a hole in it.'

Underground out of necessity

The construction of underground spaces is no sinecure, believes Benthem. 'You shouldn't build underground just because you think it's cool or extraordinary. I suppose it is more natural to build aboveground, as you don't need to remove soil first in order to create space. That's why we opt for the underground only when there's no other way.' Some people in the Netherlands, Benthem observes, feel differently: 'On the one hand you see the construction industry constantly promoting underground building, in order to get rid of loads of concrete. A good example of this, in my opinion, is the logistics system for flower transport from Aalsmeer to Schiphol. The system will only be able to take over a maximum of 10% of the aboveground transport, and can therefore never be viable. But apart from the construction lobby, you also see a certain reluctance on the part of local governments to take decisions regarding aboveground building. It's easy to say, 'Just do it underground.' That saves you the problem of altering the aboveground environment. Take the tunnel for the high-speed train, for instance, in the green heart of the Netherlands. A terribly expensive solution to a problem that – technically at least – didn't even exist. What's more, an underground solution was far riskier. I assume the risk of train accidents in the tunnel has been consciously accepted in order to eliminate a political problem.'

'Lack of space aboveground is a good reason for building underground', admits Benthem. 'But I don't believe there is so much of a space shortage in the Netherlands. You only see concentrated high-rise buildings in a very few places. We've got our office within the ring of Amsterdam, on an industrial estate with few buildings higher than two storeys. They're building a warehouse for jeans next door, for example. Thirteen metres high, admittedly, but only on one level. A warehouse for jeans! And right near the up-market Zuidas centre.' Benthem therefore sees no need for more underground building in the Netherlands. 'One exception is the North-South line', he concedes. 'Although I would rather have metros running above ground, there was no alternative. And when you opt for an underground solution, you know it has associated disadvantages.' Benthem is not keen on spending any length of time underground. 'At least, it's more pleasant aboveground. So you try to get rid of the underground character of the design as far as possible, by admitting daylight, for example, so people don't have the feeling of being shut off from the public area of the city. For the same reason, we made connections as spacious, short and well-organised as possible. No separate halls like in the old metro in Amsterdam, but column-free spaces. People have to be brought up to ground level as quickly as possible, over the shortest distance.'

Conceptual brainstorming

Benthem feels that constructional engineering firms know little about how to make things more pleasant underground. 'While we do have sufficient technical expertise for putting our heads together with the civil engineers at an early stage in the proceedings. So you shouldn't leave such tasks to those people alone. As an architect, you have to avoid only being allowed to colour the building a little bit, like a kind of aesthetic consultant. If we don't have the opportunity to intervene intensively at the pre-project stage, then we don't start such a project. I mean, that relationship is either there or it's not.' And it is the same for Benthem whether the commission is above or below ground. 'Because both kinds of assignment are the same, in principle. You don't have two different types of architect for designing underground and aboveground buildings. You see, we don't look at architecture merely as exterior design. It's also about organising the interior.' Here, Benthem is insistent: 'Some claim that underground construction assignments can be left to interior designers, as underground spaces have no exterior. Well, I simply can't agree with that.'

North-South Line
Amsterdam,
the Netherlands
Vijzelgracht Station

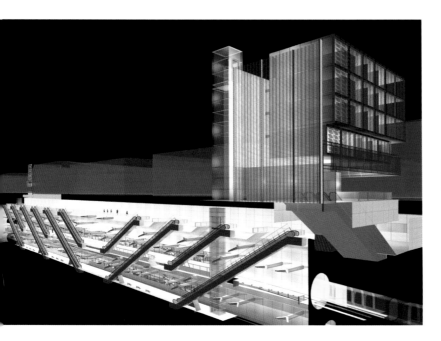

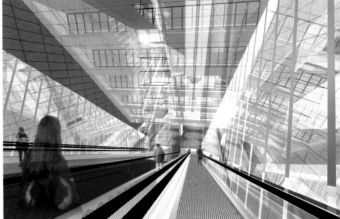

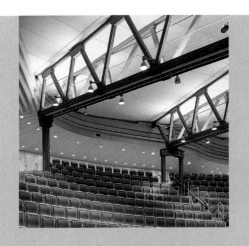

6 ENGINEERING

205

Reclaiming space from earth and water

Paul van Deelen

Philharmonic Hall Cologne

Zeeland Archives Middelburg

RECLAIMING SPACE FROM EARTH AND WATER

Subterranean constructions

Paul van Deelen

'Judge a building only once it is completely finished.' A good principle – and one that certainly applies to any underground contruction. During construction work, it is often just a shadowy underworld full of heavy equipment, puddles of water and ominous noises; it requires a lot of fantasy to imagine it ever becoming anything nice. The execution clearly shows what underground building is all about: reclaiming space from nature. Freedom of design is limited, literally, on every side, due to various environmental factors, both above and below ground level. Constructively and geotechnically, however, there are more than enough possibilities: technically, building ten storeys under the ground is perfectly feasible.

Effect of forces on an underground structure. Water and earth exercise horizontal pressure. Vertically, the water pressure forces hollow structures upwards.

The first thing the designer of an underground building is confronted with is a soil package. And water. In the Netherlands for instance, building underground generally means, in practice, building underwater. But not only here: in many other densely populated delta areas, the groundwater lies just under the surface. In order to remove earth and water and keep it at a safe distance, you first need a construction pit. Within it, a more or less normal building can subsequently be built, to form part of the box construction. Given the nature of this structure – a building in a box – an underground building differs greatly, in technical terms, from one aboveground. Which, in turn, has serious consequences for the design task.

To begin with, the interplay of forces is different, and generally far more intense than with aboveground buildings. Water and earth pressure work horizontally on an underground construction, while aboveground, wind pressure is virtually the only horizontal force. Not only gravity works vertically on an underground building, but also water pressure, which forces any hollow structure upwards, as Archimedes reasoned, just like a ship. The support construction has to resist that upward force without being pushed upward itself.

Extra weight or downward tension anchoring can keep the building in place.

A second difference can be found in the function of the building's shell. Technically speaking, it has more in common with a ship's hull than with an aboveground building. The facade, the floor and sometimes even the roof must withstand considerable water and earth pressure. Sometimes, damage from hazardous substances in the soil or groundwater has to be taken into consideration. What makes things easier, on the other hand, is that the facade need not look particularly nice from the outside, and there is naturally plenty of sound insulation and fire resistance …

In its execution, too, an underground building differs greatly from its aboveground counterpart. The interplay of forces during construction is different from what it will be in the final situation, since construction of a water- and earth-tight box requires all kinds of temporary measures. Various methods of execution are available, each imposing its own design restrictions. Characteristic of the logistics of subterranean construction is that it has to take place 'from the inside outwards,' which also affects the design. Meanwhile, neighbours will have concerns about their premises subsiding or their lives being made a misery by vibration or noise. Preventing such inconveniences is no easy task, for building underground automatically involves large quantities of equipment and materials. It is, literally, a heavy operation.

Jetgrouting a mixture of water and cement forced into the soil

Design approach

Even with an aboveground project, it is inadvisable to make a design first and then 'see later' how it might be realised. But with an underground building, such an approach will certainly fail. The forces are too strong to get around, the risks of leakage or subsidence imminent, and construction costs too high. There is no freedom of choice regarding execution methods, since the options depend largely on circumstantial factors, scale, feasible depth and form.

Underground design therefore requires a different approach from aboveground design. Different technical disciplines are involved at different stages in the process. Geotechnical and geohydrological aspects, for example, have to be taken into account from the very beginning. Structural designers and contractors play a more prominent role, just as with high-rise building.

With so much technology and so many technicians, an architect risks being reduced to a mere designer or interior architect, while the building risks becoming impractical, unpleasant or even socially unsafe. Integral design, therefore, is required. The difficult task of designing an underground building can only be performed successfully if contributions from various disciplines are kept in balance. The architect is the obvious person to supervise such a process, provided he or she has a feel for technology and does not focus too much on appearances.

Often, work is carried out according to a tripartite typology of entirely underground, partly underground or an earth-covered space, but such categories provide little real guidance, technically speaking. More useful would be a typology of integral building concepts that provided more insight into the cohesion of technical design considerations, but unfortunately nothing like it exists as yet.

Exploring possibilities

One important precondition for underground design is a detailed analysis of soil composition. The groundwater situation also requires careful investigation, since underground buildings generally stand in groundwater. In the western Netherlands, for example, one often encounters soil packages with water-repellent strata, such as clay, loam and peat (the 'Amsterdam', 'Hague' and 'Rotterdam' soil profiles), with water-bearing sand strata underneath. Such a water-repellent stratum can be used to advantage as a more or less watertight bed for a construction pit. Other soil types, e.g. the 'Utrecht profile' in the Netherlands, are missing such strata. In these sandy packages, building underground is considerably more expensive and complex, as the Delft architects' firm of Mecanoo discovered with the extension to the Andersson Elffers Felix office on Maliebaan in Utrecht. Since there was no layer of loam under the sandy soil to form a watertight box together with the sheetpile walls, the bottom first had to be sealed with hydraulic concrete and a watertight connection effected to the cellar of the existing villa. Only then could this 'swimming pool' be drained.

The effect of an underground building on the ecosystem is roughly equal to that of an aboveground building, but different in nature. Underground effects are probably greater, due to changes in groundwater flow. It is often necessary to limit the impact on groundwater flows, particularly with large or extended underground structures. At surface level, however, the changes are slighter, at least if the ecological balance above the building is restored. The earth balance is almost always negative: after construction, there is excess soil, for which a purpose needs to be found. If contaminated, it has to be disposed of. The groundwater may also be polluted, and disposing of it can require expensive measures; if so, a construction method without drainage is preferable. The disposal of construction elements at the end of the building's life can also pose problems, particularly with deep walls, injection and grouting techniques and piles cast in the ground. Sheetpile walls can be extracted; using freezing techniques, nothing remains in the soil. On the other hand, the environment can also damage a building, due to corrosive substances in the soil or groundwater; this varies greatly with location.

To achieve long life spans – which is advantageous both financially and environmentally – long-term vision is more decisive with an underground building. After all, little can be altered afterwards, as the building shell is generally water-repellent and the support floors usually take up the horizontal water and earth pressures.

THE BOWELS OF THE EARTH

We lift the heavy, round lid and cautiously insert a long ladder into a space where a tangle of intestines, blood vessels and nerves is tucked neatly out of sight under the urban epidermis. Above the noises of the street, the powerful rush of a hidden flow of water is audible. Before descending, we lower a measuring instrument to see whether it is safe. At times, the air is so poisonous it can snuff you out like a candle – a sign that we are not necessarily welcome in the guts of the city.

Now we climb down the ladder, our waders sloshing in the brown, fast-flowing sludge. This is the shadow kingdom of our civilisation, ruled by rats, who damage masonry and threaten public health. These 'minor plagues' must be regularly controlled, but efficiency is never 100%. While we may come across rats, encounters with crocodiles or snakes are highly unlikely. According to urban myth, these reptilian former pets live on here after being flushed down lavatories.

One considerable inconvenience is the size of the sewer. In films, sewers are big enough to run around in. In Dutch sewers, however, you can hardly stand upright. A few of the largest sewage pipes have diameters of 2.25 metres, but the major part of the intestinal system consists of pipes 20 to 50 centimetres across. Most sewers can therefore be seen only with the remote controlled cameras used to inspect smaller pipes.

In the past, things were very different. In some countries, they still are. The oldest sewers are the most exciting to explore. As early as the 16th century, old rivers or canals were covered for hygienic reasons. The Dieze in Den Bosch ('s-Hertogenbosch), in the Netherlands, for example, even offers boat trips, while the Zenne – for centuries a distinctive waterway in Brussels and now a nameless sewer – provides a guided tour via narrow paths. The stench of the shallow stream of faeces is not quite as bad as you would expect. But when the ooze rises to 2.6 metres, after heavy rainfall, for instance, then it is not the best place to be.

Higher demands are also made on the life-spans of materials, since inspection, maintenance and repair underground are virtually impossible. Potential alterations or extensions should be taken into account as early as possible in the design process. Extending an existing aboveground building underground is an expensive and risky proposition. If later construction is anticipated on top of an underground building, it may be worth investing in reinforced foundations. For horizontal extensions of underground structures there are no general regulations specifying maximum distances from existing buildings.

Controlling forces

The forces working on an underground building are great, so the form of the support structure has much influence on its design. To over-simplify: while the form of an aboveground building is generally determined by urban development and architectonic considerations, the form of an underground building is determined by the interplay of forces and the execution methods derived from that interplay. Some architects, among them Santiago Calatrava and Norman Foster, enjoy playing that game. The excavated arched form of Foster's metro in Bilbao, for example, renders tangible the underground forces of nature. He opposes doing everything possible to make underground spaces look as though they were aboveground.

A sturdy, watertight pit is needed to withstand the enormous horizontal (water) pressure. Since the walls have a tendency to bow inwards, both walls and floor must be thick. A lighter structure can be realised if the walls support each other by means of braces, or are anchored from behind the soil package with tension anchors. Braces need not be temporary; in Bermondsey Beacon Station on the Jubilee Line, they are clearly

The Third Man
The sewers of Vienna
Director: Orson Welles

visible as horizontal framework constructions, forming an attractive part of the architecture. It is quite common and logical to have entresols acting as braces.

Making use of forces

Instead of simply restraining these enormous forces, designers can also exploit them. A building floating like a ship in the groundwater needs less of a foundation. A good example is the bicycle parking on Amsterdam's Leidseplein, next to the Paradiso music venue. The long, narrow basement, designed by Marc Labadie, floats in groundwater. A perfect balance has been established between the upward-thrusting forces and the weight of the bicycle store, rendering foundation piles unnecessary, an instance unique in Amsterdam, which is entirely built on piles. An underground building can also be placed directly on a load-bearing layer, eliminating the need for extra foundations, in the event of subsequent aboveground additions. With a high-rise, the basement can be used to fix the core, which might be surrounded by an underground car park, for example. An underground construction can also be used during a transitional phase, transferring the forces from the building above to the foundations. Finally, an underground building can be deployed as ballast for a structure with stays, as in the case of the Erasmus Bridge in Rotterdam, where the rear stays are anchored to the bascule cellar (where the counterweight of the bridge operates).

Interesting design options are also offered by curved forms, such as spherical and cylindrical vaults, eminently suitable for taking up a substantial water and earth pressure. With round plans, for example, the horizontal force is taken up by the 'pressure ring', which forms the wall of the construction pit. This technique was used for the circular car park, with a diameter of 55 metres, under the Ossenmarkt in Groningen. Incidentally, this technique left other traces in this building, designed by Olga Architects and Ballast Nedam Engineering. The concrete earth-retaining deep wall, cast in situ, was left unfinished, and looks as though it were hewn from rock; it contrasts attractively with the geometrically shaped prefab elements composing the remainder of the building. Like the deep wall itself, the spatial organisation is also circular: a double spiral – one ramp for up-bound traffic and another for down-bound – winds around a central atrium lying 15 metres below ground level.

The box construction

Choosing the materials for a box construction is purely a question of weighing technical and financial parameters. Generally, aesthetic characteristics are unimportant, even though the walls of a construction pit do sometimes

Ossenmarkt car park
Groningen, the
Netherlands
OLGA Architecten

remain visible, as in the car park in Groningen, mentioned above. The major requirement is that the box is strong enough, resistant to its aggressive environment and, in most cases, watertight. Another factor is whether the elements play a role during construction only, or else become parts of the final building, in which case they will need to have a longer life span. For small structures, wood and plastic are sometimes suitable, but for deeper buildings the choice is mainly limited to concrete and steel, not to mention the earth itself, albeit in a processed and reinforced form.

New developments are high-strength concrete (which enables slimmer constructions), self-sealing concrete (which improves working conditions, watertightness and flexibility of form), extruded steel fibre concrete as well as improved injection techniques.

For the vertical delimitation of the construction pit, a wall can be composed of prefabricated parts (such as sheetpiling or a 'Berlin wall'), cast in the ground (for example a deep wall, screw pile wall or bentonite screen), or made by improving the existing earth body (by means of injection with gel, jet grouting, injection with a water and cement mixture or freezing). A slope is, naturally, the simplest solution, but not always suitable. In the Netherlands with its specific soil composition and ground water, and because of the limited space at most construction sites, it is rarely applicable. A slope is possible at locations like the zoo in Emmen, for example, where the soil is ideal and the groundwater level low. Ernst von Meijenfeldt designed the partly underground and partly earth-covered Maki building there. The earth from the construction pit was, incidentally, used on the roof, where the kangaroos now hop happily around.

The solutions available for the bed of the construction pit are comparable to those for the walls: a natural subsoil (possible when containing water-repellent strata of clay, loam or peat), hydraulic concrete (often anchored against upward force with tension piles or tension anchors), jet grouting, gel-injection, freezing or a membrane.

Designing the shell

In addition to its role as support, box construction also has a dividing function. Mistakenly, people often consider only structural requirements, but an aboveground building is not finished either when only the support structure is standing. The range of tools for designing the shell has yet to be fully developed. It is difficult to say which requirements the shell has to meet; these depend largely on function. For accommodations, for example, the demands on the dividing function are greater than for a car park, which can lead to an entirely different structural design and much higher costs. Technically, the shell is an awkward task. Construction is no less complex than for

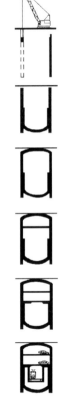

212

a normal facade or roof, but damage is more difficult to identify and almost impossible to repair. In general, shell construction proceeds from the inside outwards: first box construction, then water repelling measures (with steel sheetpile walls, the two are combined), thermal insulation, if any, and finally the support structure for the interior of the building. Opening the shell for pipes and cables, lift shafts, parts of the support construction, etc., almost always leads to complicated – and therefore expensive and risky – solutions. Fitting thermal insulation, incidentally, is no easy task; this complex problem is dealt with extensively in chapter 7.

Complete watertightness may seem a logical requirement, but in practice, it is virtually unfeasible. Still, good design and careful execution can prevent leaks due to cracks, seams and joints. Nevertheless, even with good water and damp proofing, variations in pressure mean that structures cannot usually be made entirely watertight. Steel, if properly welded, is in itself sufficiently water-repellent and damp-proof, but concrete is seldom so, especially if there are strict requirements concerning relative humidity. For the lowest floor, therefore, where pressure is highest, extra measures are needed. Small quantities of water cannot be allowed to build up in the structure, but have to evaporate on the inside. Otherwise, at low surface temperatures and with insufficient ventilation, mould soon forms. Fitting good water and damp proofing, incidentally, is easier said than done. It must always be done during construction of the shell, increasing the likelihood of damage. As yet, there is no adequate solution. Still, box-within-a-box construction, also discussed in chapter 7, is a good solution, and is the only way to achieve a good interior environment. With such construction, two very different functions – earth retention and climatisation – are divided into two separate construction elements, preferably with a ventilated cavity in between.

Sound insulation

In principle, sound insulation between an underground space and its surroundings is exceptionally high; Practically speaking, the only significant sound transfer is via entrances and exits into buildings and ventilation installations. Incidentally, good sound insulation alone is no argument for building underground; there are simpler solutions available aboveground. Good sound insulation makes underground buildings eminently suitable for functions that themselves produce a great deal of noise, such as discos, or those requiring quiet, such as concert halls or recording studios. Noise from equipment inside can be a nuisance. In a partially submerged, partially earth-covered housing project at Saint John's University in Minnesota, it is so quiet inside that when a refrigerator starts up, the noise seems annoyingly loud. High demands are therefore made on interior walls. In Cologne, unsuspecting rollerskaters caused irritating problems, for they were audible when skating on the 'roof' of an underground concert hall.

The Hague tram tunnel

However well the structural design of the box is geared to surrounding buildings, soil and groundwater, unpleasant surprises can occasionally have far-reaching consequences. That was the case with the tram tunnel in the centre of The Hague, which started to leak several times during construction. The Office for Metropolitan Architecture's complex design for the 'Souterrain' included not only tram rails but also car parks, shops and access to department stores. The structural design combines techniques similar to those used for polders with the wall-roof method. Leaks were caused primarily by the unstable soil structure. These started in 1997 with a relatively small leak, which could be sealed with gel. A year later, a leak appeared in the concrete mortar support trench, which runs between the two walls and is supposed to prevent groundwater from rising. 140,000 litres of water per hour poured into the tunnel. Flowing water washed sand in from the outside, causing subsidence, so that part of the road surface fell into the tunnel box. To remedy this, the tunnel was flooded. This seemingly contradictory measure prevented any more sand from being swept into the tunnel. Delays have lasted three years already, and costs have doubled. But there is light at the end of the tunnel – so to speak. With perseverance and ingenuity, the tunnel is finally being completed. Beginning in 2004, trams will run under Grote Marktstraat.

Execution methods
Various methods, sometimes used in combination, have been developed for underground box construction. Later we will have more to say about the choice between these methods.

The Open construction pit
This is the simplest type of construction pit. The earth is excavated, while a natural slope or an earth-retaining wall delimits the pit. The groundwater level can be temporarily lowered, if necessary, by draining. In this type of pit, the underground structure can be built in a more or less traditional manner. Depth is limited to one or two storeys. This method offers a high degree of freedom of form; the scale is limited by the degree to which the underground water permeates and the possibilities for draining. An open construction pit is not as convenient if there are other buildings in the immediate vicinity.

The Closed construction pit
The term 'closed' means that the construction pit is a more or less watertight box, keeping out groundwater. The groundwater level in the construction pit can then be lowered, while the level outside remains unchanged. The walls – retention walls or deep walls (such as cement bentonite screens), for example – reach down to a more or less watertight, horizontal stratum, such as a layer of clay. Once the building is completed, the groundwater can resume its natural course.

A depth of five to seven storeys is feasible with this method; the financial optimum is three to five storeys. Freedom of form and possibilities of scale are considerable; application abutting existing buildings is reasonably successful. This construction method is the most common; the Beurstraverse in Rotterdam, for example, was built in this manner.

The 'Polder principle'
This is actually a permanently sealed construction pit. The groundwater level within the polder – the building – is artificially lowered by drainage. Water produced by seepage and leaks is removed by a drainage system. The lowest floor can be executed very simply, with clinker paving, for example. The underground car park at the RAI exhibition centre in Amsterdam was executed in this way.

The feasible depth is limited to six storeys or fewer, depending on the vertical balance of the soil. The financial optimum is three to five storeys. This relatively simple, quick construction method is reasonably suitable for use adjacent to existing buildings. The freedom of form depends only on the possibilities offered by the delimitation of the construction pit. In the Netherlands, the scale is limited by the maximum quantity of ground-

Open construction pit

Closed construction pit

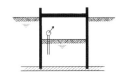

Polder principle

water that can be withdrawn according to the levels laid down by the Dutch Ground Water Act. The car park under Museumplein in Amsterdam and the railway station in Rijswijk, for example, are built according to this polder principle.

The Wall-roof method

After installing the walls – sheetpile walls or deep walls, for example – the 'roof' (actually the floor) is fitted at ground level. Then the earth underneath is excavated. Draining or excess air pressure under the roof lowers the groundwater level temporarily. In the meantime, building or refurbishment can begin on the roof. Disturbances to life aboveground can be kept as brief as possible. For that reason, this method is primarily applied in inner city areas, such as the tram tunnel in The Hague. The method is best suited to cramped building sites and constructions directly adjacent to existing buildings. Scale and depth are roughly the same as for a closed construction pit and the freedom of form depends only on the possibilities offered by the construction pit delimitation.

Caisson method

With this method, the underground structure is built elsewhere as a closed box with a fixed form. This can be done at ground level, directly above the site for which it is destined. It is then referred to as a 'pneumatic caisson'. By spraying out the soil underneath and removing it, the caisson settles automatically into place. The groundwater level between the two cutting edges on the bottom is temporarily lowered by means of air overpressure. Parts of the first metro tunnel in Amsterdam were built in this way, as was the vast 60 metre long, 30 metre wide and 10 metre high basement under the Ministry of Defence in the centre of The Hague. With pneumatic caissons, safety aspects during construction require extra attention, particularly for workers in the area underneath who are spraying away the soil. The freedom of form and scale are limited to approximately 2,000 m², as the entire structure has to retain its shape. A depth of up to five to ten storeys can be achieved. A caisson can also be shipped in via a temporary canal, and sunk into place. Much experience with this method has been gained in the Netherlands, where most tunnels under rivers are built in this way. In the 1960s, the Coolsingel Canal in Rotterdam temporarily looked like a real transport canal when caissons were being shipped along it for the metro tube. The Amsterdam Central Station on the North-South metro line will also be executed as a sunken caisson. The caisson method is quite suitable for cramped building locations and extremely advantageous for use next to existing buildings, as the groundwater level in the surroundings is unaffected. For this reason, the method was also once proposed for an underground concert hall under the Parade in Den Bosch. Despite a positive feasibility study and accompanying risk analysis, the project was never carried out, for fear of damage to the historic surroundings and, in particular, the Sint-Jan cathedral.

Drilling

Strictly speaking, drilling is truly authentic 'underground building': not only is the structure itself placed under the ground, but the construction process also takes place underground. The advantages are evident: construction proceeds virtually unnoticed. In other words 'not in my backyard' is here carried to the extreme. Only where the drilling machine comes and goes can anything be seen at ground level. A bucket wheel excavator at the front of the drilling machine loosens the earth. The surrounding earth directly behind the excavator is supported temporary by the outside of the tunnel drilling machine (the shield), inside which a tunnel wall (the lining) is constructed, generally from prefabricated concrete elements. Injection or freezing techniques can be used to limit the impact on the immediate surroundings.

Drilling offers little freedom of form, which makes the method really suitable only for infrastructure. The cross section is, in principle, always round, with an equal diameter throughout the entire stretch of between three and

214

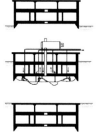

A pneumatic caisson is built at ground level. When the earth underneath is sprayed away, it sinks into place.

no more than circa fourteen metres, and the drill can make only slight curves. In Japan, small-scale experiments are already being carried out with other types of combined cross sections. The installation of a drill is so complicated that drilling only pays off on longer stretches. All this makes drilling particularly suitable for new infrastructure in complex situations, in densely populated or sensitive areas. Unlike elsewhere, the drilling technique was, for some time, rarely applied in the Netherlands, as traditional methods – particularly sinking caissons – were successful and efficient. The Second Heinenoord Tunnel was the first drilled tunnel in the Netherlands. After its successful execution, the principle was employed for the Botlek and Sophia railway tunnels and the Pannerdensch Canal Tunnel (sections of the Betuwe Line), the Groene Hart tunnel (part of the High Speed Train Link South) and the Westerschelde Tunnel. For construction of the North-South Line in Amsterdam, major parts of the line under the historic inner city will be drilled out. This illustrates the success of the method, which is now being applied to many projects that could not otherwise have been executed in the Netherlands. The architects firm of Zwarts & Jansma made grateful use of the drilling technique for the Second Heinenoord Tunnel. Large construction pits were needed for the construction and operation of the drill, and these now form vast entrance halls, with ample room for lifts, escalators and a great deal of daylight. Together with the high level of finishing, these halls contribute to social safety.

Developing methods

Various methods are currently under development that combine the advantages of drilling (practically no disturbance at ground level) with a greater range of forms. Ideas such as 'GIA' and 'Geo-domes' are prime examples. The GIA concept is based on a large underground space taking the form of a kind of concrete sphere. Geo-domes are vaulted halls with diameters of 100 metres or more. Not only can an entire football stadium fit inside one, but many other kinds of other functions as well, such as exhibition halls, sports halls, music venues and shopping centres. The idea is to install them below existing infrastructure, in other words at least 50 metres under ground level. The large dimensions are made possible by the dome shape, which can withstand the pressure of the surrounding earth and water with relatively thin walls. Supported by a number of private entrepreneurs, the Amsterdam municipal engineering office is focussing on the development of Geo-domes. The idea has been around since the 1980s, and a test dome has been built in Japan.

Choosing between execution methods

The execution method best suited to a specific task depends on a large number of criteria. These are, in turn, derived from the construction time available, the budget, the building design (scale, depth, plan and complexity), the composition of the soil and requirements set by surrounding buildings. The weight each criterion carries varies from case to case, as can be seen clearly in the construction of metro lines through inner city area. Here, a pneumatic caisson, there a piece of wall-roof method, then a sunken caisson. Roughly speaking, the highest costs per square metre (approximately ten storeys deep, built according to the caisson method) are around double the least expensive ones (approximately four storeys deep, with closed construction pit and sheet pile walls). Additional underground storeys do not necessarily increase the price per square metre; if an expensive sheetpile wall has to be installed anyway, you might as well realise as much floor surface as possible.

Open construction pits are simple and relatively inexpensive, but only where it is possible to draw off and discharge groundwater. Legislation may forbid this, since the effects of drying can make large-scale removal of groundwater damaging to the environment. Lowering of groundwater levels can also cause sinking and damage wooden foundations. For constructing car parks and similar structures under existing buildings, it is more or less standard to use a closed construction pit, surrounded by a steel sheet pile wall. Under normal circumstances, this method of execution offers the best price/quality ratio. For a car park with several storeys under ground

Second Heinoord Tunnel
Rotterdam, the Netherlands
Zwarts & Jansma

level, a 'polder' can be a good solution, since it is quick to build, at least if the soil has a water-repellent stratum. The rather expensive wall-roof method is appealing if ground level functions can be interrupted for a short period only. While construction is progressing underground, normal life can recommence on the 'roof'. If an underground building has to be realised immediately adjacent to existing ones, then strict requirements will apply in the area affected by the nuisance due to noise, vibration and fear of subsidence. The relatively expensive caisson method is then perhaps the best choice, since it is, in principle, also unnecessary to enter the premises of adjacent properties, either above or below ground level, or to reinforce the foundations of neighbouring buildings.

Safety

Due to several fundamental differences between conditions above and below ground level respectively, what is safe up above is not necessarily safe down below. First of all, disasters are more difficult to detect from a distance. Substances heavier than air collect at lower levels, so leaks of, for example, water or poisonous gasses can long remain undetected. Fire extinguishing water also collects there. Another effect of the underground location is that escape and emergency aid must proceed from the inside out. There are no windows to break in order to get out or, indeed, in. This fact means high demands on the quality and capacity of escape routes, safe places and access for emergency services. Furthermore, escape routes from underground buildings run, in principle, upward, which also has consequences. People are therefore moving in the same direction as fire and smoke. And running upstairs takes more time than running downstairs; older and less able people may not make it to the top. On the other hand, one advantage of underground buildings is that fires spread more slowly there, since, in general, less oxygen can enter.

Globally speaking, safety approaches for underground buildings do not differ from those aboveground. Safety has to be approached in an 'integrated' fashion, as specialist publications emphasise; individual measures will not suffice. First comes a definition of the desired level of safety, which depends on function. Here, the relevant factors are the numbers of people inside, their degree of familiarity with the building, and the quantity of inflammable materials present. The second step is to determine which dangers are present, and the likelihood of their actually materialising. Dangers may include fire, explosion, stupefaction, gassing or suffocation, flood, collapse, social insecurity, crime or terrorism and a breakdown of functions. These dangers are incorporated into scenarios that establish hypothetically possible chains of events and effects. The necessary measures can be derived from the representative scenarios. One scenario may help establish the quantity of water needed to extinguish fires, another the width of escape routes, and so forth.

Even an objectively safe building can be perceived as unsafe. Such perceptual questions are dealt with extensively in chapter 5. On the other hand, even in a building that is perceived as safe, emergency services personnel can lose their way during emergencies, unable to get their bearings (as happened once to the fire brigade during a fire in the car park under Amsterdam's Town Hall).

Although objective safety is a basic function of physical characteristics, subjective safety depends more on a building's spatial qualities: a surveyable, spacious structure, extended vistas, absence of blind corners and abundant daylight. Another illustration of the fact that technical and architectural designers really cannot do without each other.

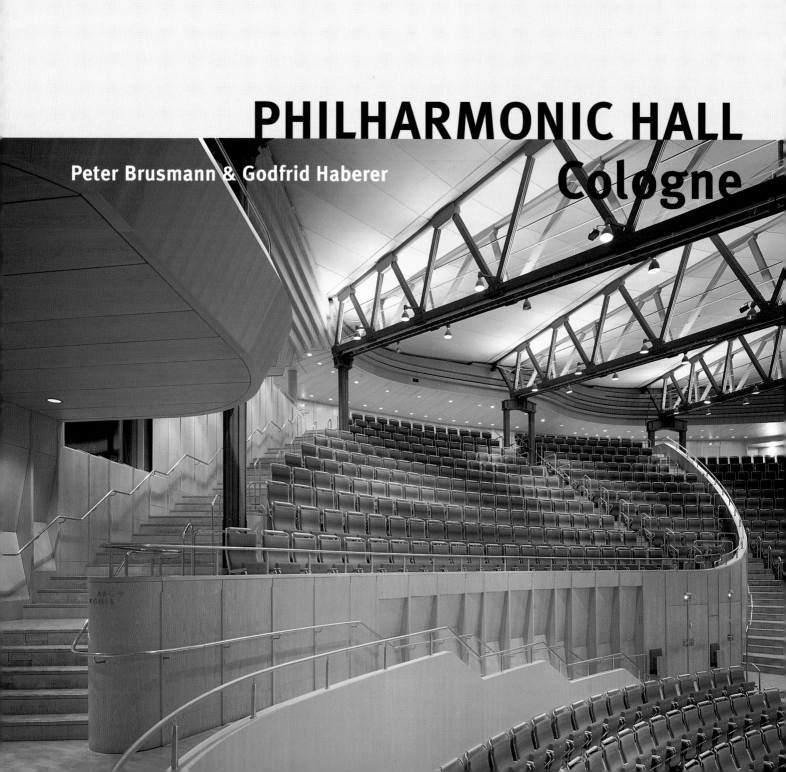

PHILHARMONIC HALL
Cologne

Peter Brusmann & Godfrid Haberer

KÖLNER PHILHARMONIE

Function **concert hall**

Address **Cathedral Square/Rhine**

Promenade, Cologne, Germany

Hall volume **21,000 m³**

Depth **25 metres**

Number of levels underground **1**

Construction time **6 years**

Initiative **1976**

Design **1976**

Construction **1980-1986**

Client **Kölner Philharmonie**

Architects **Peter Brusmann, Godfrid**

Haberer, Cologne

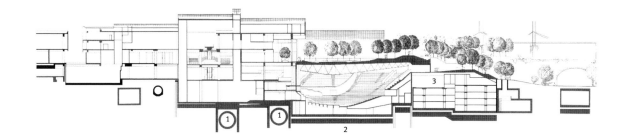

Cologne Philharmonic

Longitudinal section

1 Metro

2 Concert hall

3 Car park

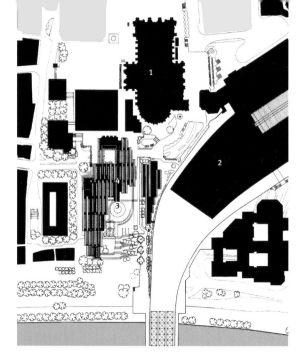

Cologne Philharmonic Site plan

1 Cathedral

2 Station

3 Cologne Philharmonic

4 Wallraf Richartz Museum/

Museum Ludwig

Cologne Philharmonic
Concert hall

In older inner cities, the wish to condense and add new functions while upgrading existing ones is creating favourable conditions for underground construction. In Cologne, the political will to revitalise the decaying inner city led to the Altstadt/Dom/Rhein project, a master plan encompassing the old city, the cathedral and the banks of the Rhine.

Various parts of the ard project were realised underground. The road along the banks of the Rhine was moved to a tunnel approximately 750 metres long, with two three-lane roads. A five-storey car park and a concert hall seating 2000 were also built underground. By planning these functions both underground and as close as possible to the nearby museums and the foundations of the cathedral, it was possible to create a wide open space at surface level that slopes down from the cathedral to the Rhine promenade. Proximity to the Rhine made it impossible to lower the groundwater level by means of drainage. To prevent problems with groundwater, construction was carried out in gigantic pits that had been sealed with concrete or steel walls and an impermeable concrete floor. These support elements would later become the load-bearing structures of the buildings themselves.

Located between the Dom Passage and the Rhine promenade, the concert hall of the Kölner Philharmonie lies partly under the Museum Ludwig and partly beneath a former bus station. The open area above has been developed into a lively town square. Together with the Wallraf-Richartz Museum, the Museum Ludwig, and Cologne Cathedral, the concert hall forms a large-scale cultural complex on the Rhine. Entrances to the most important functions are situated on the square, while access to the concert hall is set apart from the museum entrances. After entering, visitors find themselves in a lavishly decorated complex of passages surrounding the hall.

The route into the concert hall itself is illuminated by bright overhead lighting, giving the impression of being separated from the outside only by the roof. The hall takes the form of an amphitheatre, and offers no sense of its relation to the world outside and above ground. A strong artificial light, reminiscent of the skylight in the Pantheon, illuminates the centre of the domed ceiling.

Finished with tiles, the roof of the concert hall forms part of a public square, its presence indicated by a circular pattern in the paving. If it had been realised above ground, drastic measures would have been required to prevent noise disturbance from the nearby railway line, road traffic and transport over the Rhine. While the site rendered these unnecessary, contact sound from the square has proved audible in the hall. Consequently, skateboarding is forbidden during performances.

ZEELAND ARCHIVES
Middelburg

Benthem Crouwel Architects

Zeeland Archives

Section

1 Terrace

2 Archives

3 Café

4 Study area

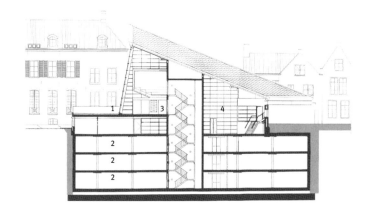

ZEELAND ARCHIVES

Function **storage**

Address **Hofplein 16, Middelburg,**

the Netherlands   225

Floor surface underground **4,200 m²**

Floor surface above ground **1,200 m²**

Depth **13 metres**

Number of levels underground **3**

Construction time **2 years**

Design **1994-1997**

Construction **1997-1999**

Client **Dutch Government Buildings Agency,**

south west department, Schiedam

Architects **Benthem Crouwel Architects,**

Amsterdam

Engineers **Arcadis Bouw Infra BV, The Hague**

Zeeland Archives
Study area

When the Archives of the province of Zeeland were combined with the municipal archives of Middelburg and Veere to form the new Zeeland Archives, they required 25 linear kilometres of archive storage in all. A manor house in Middelburg was placed at the disposal of the Archives's management by the Buildings Agency of the Dutch Government. When the Van de Perrehuis, a major national monument dating from 1765, proved far too small, an expansion was clearly indicated. Since the grounds were far from large, the solution was obvious: the Archives would have to go underground.

The Zeeland Archives welcomed the renovations and restoration as a means to shake off their stuffy image. The point of departure for Benthem Crouwel, the firm commissioned with the new building, was to create an open, modern building with a clear, well-organised structure. There would be aboveground space for the public, and three underground depots for archival documents.

Zeeland Archives

Site plan,

ground floor plan

1 New building

2 Archive café

3 Terrace

4 Garden

5 Offices

6 Genealogical centre

7 Atrium study area

8 Photographic studio

9 Reception

10 Waiting room

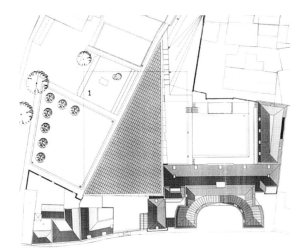

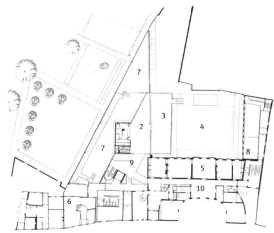

Levels -1/ -2/ -3

Plan of new building

1 Atrium

2 Lift

3 Entrance to archive

4 Watertight airlock

5 Archive

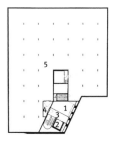

Zeeland Archives

Atrium with three levels

of archives

The stately Van de Perrehuis is situated in one of the few mediaeval areas untouched by the ravages of World War II, and Benthem Crouwel had to approach this special, historical environment with the utmost care. With its triangular shape, the new building in the courtyard follows the contours of a mediaeval alleyway. A public footpath alongside the new building leads to the city centre.

Architecturally, the new building contrasts strikingly with its historic surroundings. A historic gate, formerly opening onto the courtyard, leads directly into the heart of the building. The building's transparent structure is revealed at a glance. On a plateau several steps higher are the reception area and the Archives's cafe, with its open air terrace. The cylindrical volume of the auditorium hangs high in the air; the reading room is visible below. An atrium affords a view thirteen metres into the ground, showing three identical levels. Here, the Zeeland Archives's most precious possessions are housed. In the reading room, situated above the 'treasure chamber' and looking onto the courtyard garden, visitors can request access to stored archive documents.

During construction of the new building, the Van de Perrehuis was also thoroughly restored and adapted as office space for personnel. The original building and new section are seamlessly connected. Personnel walking from the old building to the new one have the impression of fast forwarding two centuries in an imaginary time machine: from 18th century romanticism to contemporary high-tech.

The new building, designed to house precious historical materials, is equipped with an air purification system, and maintained at a temperature of 17.9°C, with the correct atmospheric humidity (51 percent relative humidity). To prevent a disaster should the former island of Walcheren become flooded – something likely to occur once every 4000 years, according to the Department of Public Works – all accesses to the underground depots are fitted with water-resistant doors. The depots are located nine metres below groundwater level. To achieve the desired climatic conditions, walls must be both water-resistant and damp-proof. For that reason, the fully welded, seventeen-metre-deep sheetpiling was constructed as a permanent formwork. Once the sheetpiling was installed, the construction pit was allowed to fill with water as soil was excavated; in order to avoid subsidence of other foundations in the area, the groundwater level was prevented from falling. A hydraulic concrete working platform one metre thick was poured into the swimming pool thus created.

228

Zeeland Archives
Study area

Divers checked the soil beforehand to remove any irregularities, such as lumps of peat. Once the construction pit had been pumped out, the sheetpiling was entirely welded up from bottom to top and the construction wall cast directly against the steel, creating a damp-proof structure. The underground construction is made entirely of concrete, upon which rest the steel columns supporting the triangular roof. The aboveground section is of steel and glass. Sturdy construction and innovative use of materials relegate the stuffy, old-fashioned image of the historical archive irrevocably to the past.

Pioneer of the underground

Interview with John Carmody

The use of underground space in contemporary architecture is nothing new. As early as the 1970s, John Carmody and Ray Sterling from the American Underground Space Center in Minneapolis, Minnesota, focussed attention on the systematic development of underground space as a solution to urban space shortages. When the American people were hit by an oil embargo in 1973, creating the financial impetus for energy-saving living, earth-covered houses enjoyed a certain popularity. That interest in saving energy has returned in recent years. Sustainable building is now an all-embracing objective, which can also be achieved underground. Carmody hopes that, this time, interest will take root.

Although John Carmody graduated as an architect, he never felt the need to manipulate the environment with his own designs – at least not directly. But he did want to leave an indirect mark on the architecture and urban development of North America. As co-director with Raymond Sterling, of the Underground Space Center (a former knowledge centre affiliated with the Department of Civil & Mineral Engineering of the University of Minnesota in Minneapolis), he has been inventorying possible uses for underground space since the 1970s. 'It was an initiative of the mining engineer, Charles Fairhurst', says Carmody, explaining the centre's origins. 'He felt it was important for urban developers and architects to realise that, with the systematic application of mining techniques, an extra level could be added underneath the city, without having to break up ground level. That underground space right under the city can be made suitable for all manner of functions.' From a geological point of view, Minneapolis and many other American cities have the right kind of underground for excavating subterranean space in such a way. Despite all kinds of discussions and plans, however, few underground projects have been realised, which Carmody finds regrettable: 'The thing is, on a larger, urban scale, you can achieve really significant advantages. It's a way of concentrating building. People don't need to travel long distances and you prevent the city swallowing up the surrounding countryside.'

Pressure on space

Both in Minneapolis or in North America as a whole, little use is being made of the underground on a large scale. 'That's not how the political system works here', says Carmody. 'You need a dictator to put plans like that into action'. North American governments are playing something of a waiting game vis a vis underground construction projects. Initiatives come from project developers or conglomerates of private entrepreneurs, who study the cost-effectiveness of underground projects individually. Very few master plans have been drawn up for underground projects in major cities such as Montreal and Toronto, which have considerable underground networks.
The Canadian government encourages only pedestrian connections between different construction projects, both underground or aboveground. The skyway systems in Minneapolis and Edmonton are prime examples. The underground connections are sometimes little more than tunnels, and sometimes attractively laid out

shopping arcades. 'The lack of a master plan means that labyrinth-like constructions are appearing, in which you can wander forever', says Carmody. 'Street level is losing its significance. In cities with long, cold winters, in particular, pedestrians choose the underground networks in preference to the street. This is degrading street level to an open traffic sewer without any incentive to linger'.

Exploitation of the underground in America has a primarily economic basis, which is why underground intensification only occurs where the pressure on space is high: in inner cities and on university campuses, where some fine examples can be found. A number of underground buildings have been realised on the campus of the University of Minnesota in Minneapolis, of which the Civil & Mineral Engineering Building, in particular, is striking. For several years, the lowest office level of this building, 35 metres under ground, accommodated the Underground Space Center, where Carmody carried out a great deal of research into the human aspects of underground space. In his view, the greatest barrier to the use of underground spaces is psychological. In his book, *Underground Space Design* (1993), Carmody lays down a set of design guidelines he has applied in practice in the Civil and Mineral Engineering Building. Many experiments in the area of daylight and artificial light have been conducted in the building. Daylight is transported to the deepest levels by a complex optical instrument, which protrudes above the building like a kind of periscope. Planning views was less successful. Nevertheless, deep under ground, they managed to realise a kind of window with a view of the environment above ground.

Earth-covered houses

The earlier popularity of earth-covered houses – another use of underground space researched by the Underground Space Center – can be explained as a direct consequence of the 1973 oil embargo. Energy costs rose staggeringly. 'And with the price rises grew interest in innovations in the areas of passive and active solar energy', says Carmody. 'Underground building and, in particular, earth-covered buildings with a southern aspect, turned out to save a great deal of energy. We, too, switched our attention from mining underground space to houses in or at ground level (partially) covered with earth. Our first book on the subject, *Earth Sheltered Housing Design*, sold some 300,000 copies worldwide in eight or ten different languages. Which is incredible, because the study wasn't all that professional. But the demand for information on experiments with earth-covered houses was enormous. Some people saw building houses in this manner as a way of surviving. They wanted an autarkic place where you are not dependent on energy. If there's a power cut in an earth-covered house, you're not going to freeze so easily.'

Civil & Mineral
Engineering Building
Minneapolis, USA
BRW Architects

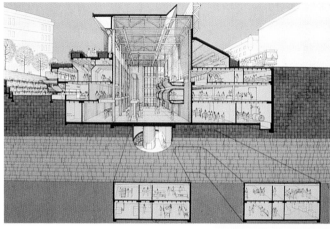

All the same, Carmody feels, earth-covered buildings remained the preserve of an elite of moneyed pioneers. 'A lot of people built their own homes', he continues, 'but they didn't always do it so well. There were no computer models, no advanced methods for calculating a building. Sometimes, roofs even starting leaking while they were still building, incurring extra costs.' The American real estate market, already rather conservative in Carmody's eyes, was not exactly enthusiastic about such experimentation, making it almost impossible for less affluent private individuals to acquire earth-covered homes. 'After all, the bank isn't easily going to grant a mortgage if no real estate agent has any confidence in being able to sell your house.' Underground living finally died out when energy costs started to stabilise in the early 1980s, limiting the necessity for energy-conscious living. 'Besides, we learned to build energy-saving houses that didn't differ radically from the norm', says Carmody.

Sustainable building

Since the end of the 1980s, there has been a noticeable renewal in enthusiasm for underground living. 'Houses with grass roofs are starting to appear again', says Carmody. 'But technology has changed. There is more focus on the supporting construction of the roofs, which, in turn, can be made far lighter, thanks to new building methods from Europe.' The reason for opting for grass roofs has also changed. 'Grass roofs not only help keep a check on the city's energy consumption; they also absorb rainwater, so you don't need an extensive drainage system. What's more, I think it's much better to retain water for the environment and let it sink, so the soil is cleansed. A natural function we didn't utilise before.'

The new earth-covered houses are inspired by the idea of sustainable building. 'Unlike in the 1970s, when we tended towards an extremely limited interpretation of design and saw a house more as a machine for saving energy, we now take into account more factors than the environment alone', explains Carmody. 'We also consider the perception and well-being of the inhabitants and the relationship of a building with the surrounding buildings.' Aesthetics and environmental awareness now go hand in hand. That is probably why, in contrast to the 1970s, a lot of architects are becoming interested in environmentally aware construction. 'You see a lot of them adopting the principle of sustainable building and the philosophy behind it,' says Carmody. 'They are taking into consideration the land, the water, the energy consumption, the people who live in the buildings and their health, the use of materials and their influence on the environment.'

Carmody is a great advocate of sustainable building, which is why the research centre he now runs is called the Center of Sustainable Building Research. By analysing completed projects, the institute, which is affiliated with the University of Minnesota, is endeavouring to improve the quality of sustainable building. 'What we want to achieve is more comprehensively integrated sustainable design. Because we now know more about how we live on this planet and what impact our buildings and cities have on the environment,' says Carmody. 'I've always been optimistic and I think that, one day, people will wake up and say that we have to make our buildings more sustainable. That we don't need to spend our money on bombing the Middle East to secure our hold on the oil reserves. It's the idea that this will one day happen that keeps me going. But what bothers me is that architects in America see sustainable building not as an ethical issue, but as a design principle. Something that goes in and out of style. Unlike Europe, where renowned architects, such as Renzo Piano, are really trying to change the impact of building on the environment.'

Underground building as a tool

For Carmody, underground building is one of the architect's tools for designing sustainable buildings: 'The most important thing is to try and place the right functions underground. I see no reason why a school, hospital, office or any other place where people spend a lot of time should be underground. We shouldn't force people to spend time underground, only to compensate them for missing the outside world with clever design tricks. But you can certainly accommodate other functions underground, such as bookshops or museums, where people spend relatively short periods of time. After all, these are places where there are often no windows, anyway.'

When asked for an example of the good use of underground space, Carmody cites the work of Gunnar Birkerts. He has proved himself a master of subterranean construction in the underground libraries of the Cornell University in New York and the University of Michigan in Ann Arbor. 'Birkerts manages to transport daylight into the deeper levels in a fabulous way and gives buildings with limited visibility a strong presence'. As a less powerful example, Carmody cites the Walker library in Minneapolis. 'The building is situated in an area with a low concentration of office buildings and the roof is used as a car park', he says. 'In such a context, the fact that this building has been constructed underground is completely incomprehensible. On the other hand, if it were situated on a campus or anywhere else where a historic environment needs protecting, then it would be easier to see such a library as a good example of the use of underground space.' Because Carmody fully understands that not only function, but also context can be a major reason for realising a building underground. 'The integration of the underground into a design must not be an objective in itself', he states. 'After all, you can hardly imagine someone saying, "I want to construct an underground building. Where shall I put it?"'

233

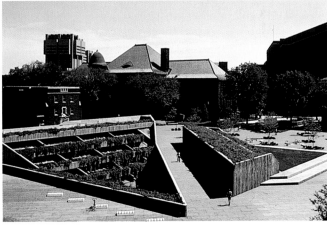

Williamson Hall,
university bookshop
Minneapolis, USA
BRW Architects

ENERGY AND INTERIOR CLIMATE

Buildings like icebergs Ed Melet

Two housing projects: Nine Houses Dietikon

Soft and Hairy House Tsukuba City

Two libraries: Law Faculty library Ann Arbor

Marriott Library Salt Lake City

BUILDINGS LIKE ICEBERGS

Healthy, energy-efficient underground construction

Ed Melet

In the 1970s, industrial parks filled with shiny office behemoths sprouted up like mushrooms. It seemed the ideal situation, the emergence of an artificial working environment. Machines would closely monitor interior climates to the tenth of a degree, while the tinted glass would keep out daylight and insure views. All too soon, however, such environments proved not to be particularly user-friendly. Due to the monotony of a constant temperature and atmospheric humidity and the twilight effect of the tinted glass, people did not feel well in these 'sick buildings'. Similar claustrophobic effects are a hazard of underground buildings, as well. The environment in itself feels more hostile, which is why, in creating the interior climate, an attempt must be made to bring as many natural elements inside as possible, including a maximum of daylight and of natural ventilation. Not only can a pleasant climate be created, but, by making use of the coolness of the earth, a great amount of energy can be saved.

In central Europe, the climate makes it difficult to arrive at a single ready-made, energy-efficient solution for controlling the climate in 'ordinary' aboveground buildings. It is warm in the summer and quite cold in the winter. To reduce energy consumption, the emphasis is on limiting heat loss. Buildings are therefore wrapped in thick layers of insulating material, and their sparse openings fitted with insulating glass. This type of facade is inconvenient during the summer, since, in addition to the heat production inside, the sun heats up the buildings more than ever. Well-insulated facades prevent heat from escaping easily or quickly, and it tends to build up inside. Despite the increasing quality of glass and outdoor blinds that are fitted with increasing frequency, air conditioners are still necessary to prevent uncontrolled heating, and they consume a great deal of energy.

Underground, the exterior climate plays little or no role. Due to the insulating effect of the earth, the underground temperature fluctuates between 8 and 12° Celsius all year round. The dimensioning of facades in such a stable climate is relatively simple and, in view of the heat problem in intensively used buildings, it would seem sensible to make use of the coolness of the earth. Cooling then becomes superfluous and substantial energy savings therefore easy to achieve. Incidentally, this method is not exactly new. Ancient Greek colonists built caves behind their houses on Santorini Island, Greece. During the summer, the cool rooms at the back of the house could be used and, in the cooler months, they could enjoy the autumn sun in the rooms at the front. The inhabitants of Guadix in Spain sill carve their homes from the ground in order to benefit from both the coolness and the warmth of the earth.

Lack of comfort and coolness

In terms of energy, the use of underground space appears to be economical, but it also has its disadvantages. Central Europe tends to have higher standards of comfort than either the Ancient Greeks or southern Europe. Without preventative measures, the walls and floors of an underground building take on the temperature of the soil and make the rooms cold. Such cold surfaces are perceived as extremely unpleasant. Furthermore, relative humidity in these rooms will be extremely high, with possible condensation as a result. Such conditions are ideal for fungi, which spread a musty smell, not exactly adding to the appeal of such spaces.

It is relatively easy to take measures to prevent this cold penetration. The principle is similar to the one involved in insulating ordinary buildings: a layer of insulating material can simply be fitted against the walls and floors to stop heat from escaping.

Another method for avoiding cold surfaces is to warm the substratum with hot water or install wall and floor heating. The last two methods seem to enjoy an extra advantage: the surrounding earth is warmed and, although

237

Rock dwellings
in Andalusia
Guadix, Spain

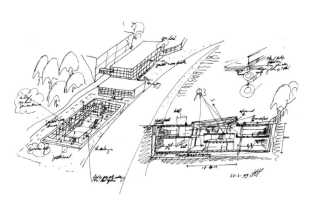

Extension to the Art Academy

Arnhem, the Netherlands

Hubert-Jan Henket

the influence of the flowing groundwater is an unknown factor, a stable situation is soon achieved. The earth reaches practically the same temperature as the interior space, which means that surfaces in the underground building will not become cold again, even without heating. This strictly limits heat loss from the rooms, and far less energy is therefore needed for heating. The problem remains that there is no stable situation in the rooms themselves. Everything we do produces heat: lighting, machines such as coffeemakers, refrigerators, photo-copiers and computers. Additionally, we ourselves radiate a great deal of heat. Furthermore, we need daylight to function properly, especially in places used intensively for long periods of time, such as offices and classrooms. Daylight is more dynamic than artificial light. It has more contrast, which appears to be crucial to our wellbeing. It stimulates our brains, increasing alertness and making us feel better. 'Sick buildings' illustrate just how impor-tant daylight is. Dark-tinted glass might keep out the heat of the sun, but at the same time, it gives users a clouded vision of their surroundings. This produces a very unpleasant, shut-in feeling. Hence the importance of admitting as much unadulterated daylight as possible, especially in underground buildings, whose locations alone can have disturbing psychological effects. But a great deal of heat enters along with daylight, heat that is both unneeded and difficult to evacuate from the complex. Solar heat must therefore be filtered out of the day-light in some fashion, yet without reducing the quality of the light.

Two 'enlightening' examples

In the Centre de conférence Usinor-Sacilor in Saint-Germain-en-Laye, the French architect, Dominique Perrault, solved this problem in an extraordinary fashion. He placed a number of underground congress halls next to a

Centre de conférence
Usinor-Sacilor
Saint-Germain-en-Laye,
France
Dominique Perrault

239

historic building, with the public spaces under a glass plate covered by a shallow layer of water. On the one hand, the water ensures absorption of solar heat, while on the other, sufficient 'distorted' light enters the underground section because of refraction of the light by the water. In his design for the Faculty Theatre of the Arnhem Art Academy, Hubert-Jan Henket solved the dilemma of how to simultaneously admit daylight and exclude solar heat in a slightly more pragmatic – and therefore far cheaper – manner. This building, with classrooms and a small theatre, was not built underground due to lack of space, but it would have seriously damaged the landscape if it had been realised aboveground. Moreover, it would have concealed the Arnhem Academy – a national monument and one of Gerrit Rietveld's most beautiful post-war buildings – from view. Henket therefore designed an underground space with a glass-roofed atrium, surrounded by classrooms. As horizontal glass surfaces are more effective than vertical ones – because light can enter unimpeded by objects – more than enough daylight penetrates deep into the building. Inside the sloping parts of the glass roof, aluminium-covered curtains will be hung, which admit plenty of light while absorbing solar gain. Nevertheless, too much heat will be produced in this building to guarantee a pleasant interior climate without extra measures.

Cooling

Superfluous heat, therefore, must somehow be removed from the building. Transferring the heat into the environment would seem the simplest solution, but this is even more awkward than in aboveground buildings. If the heat is pumped into the surrounding earth, it will heat the soil, which will reach the temperature of the emitted heat. Not only will it then be practically impossible to continue to discharge heat from the building, but there will be a risk of heat radiating inwards, making the interior climate more difficult to control. Mechanical cooling is the most obvious alternative. This is, however, conceptually speaking, a rather unsatisfactory solution, since such devices use a lot of energy, cancelling any apparent energy advantage of building underground. When a well-insulated, mechanically climatised building is placed in the ground, closed off from its surroundings, it does not benefit from the stable temperature of the surroundings, in other words of the earth itself. Energetically, such a building would be better built aboveground. Climatisation may require as much energy as an ordinary, completely sealed building, but construction itself uses far more energy. Ways have to be found, therefore, to benefit from the climatologically favourable subterranean environment, while, at the same time, attempting to create a pleasant, varied climate.

Natural ventilation

In recent decades, experiments have been carried out with natural ventilation in aboveground buildings. Unfortunately, entering currents are often either too cold or too warm and effect the interior climate negatively. Buffers are therefore used to temper this effect. In summer, for example, air is first cooled by passing it through an earth channel. In winter, the air enters the offices via a double skin facade, where it is warmed. Such systems, at once simple and ingenious, make cooling and heating superfluous for part of the year. Within fixed margins, natural ventilation generally permits users to determine the temperature and atmospheric humidity in their own rooms. The exercise of such individualized control on interior climate appears to be a crucial component of thermal comfort. Natural ventilation, furthermore, creates a less artificial climate. Like tedious artificial light, a overly static interior climate has a soporific effect on users.

The Limburg Archives

The effective use of natural ventilation is illustrated by the underground archive rooms of the Limburg Archives in Maastricht. Installing this function underground meant that nothing had to be built in the lovely courtyard of this historic complex. Moreover, the requirements for such a complex match the advantages of subterranean building almost perfectly. Temperature and humidity fluctuations must be minimised, an effect promoted by the body of the building and the surrounding grounds. Night ventilation is sufficient, partly because the structure was wrapped in an 8 mm-thick layer of HDPE foil, which prevents moisture from penetrating the building.

Lower evening temperatures promote night-time ventilation by means of cool evening air, which absorbs heat produced during the day and expels it. In the mornings, the building is cooled and ready to absorb heat again. In this context, it is important that a building has a mass appropriate to absorb enough heat. Cool evening air can be drawn in by either natural or mechanical means. The great advantage of natural ventilation is that it uses no energy, but it is highly dependent on weather conditions. If there is no wind, for example, there will be little or no air exchanged. As a result, the building will not cool down enough in the evenings. creating risks of uncontrolled warming during the day. A combination of mechanical and natural ventilation, as used in the Limburg Archives, is therefore recommended. In the event of unfavourable weather conditions, cooler outside air can be sucked in mechanically.

In Limburg, the night-time ventilation system is so efficient it renders other forms of ventilation or dehumidification unnecessary. In most other underground buildings, however, such uncomplicated types of natural ventilation will be insufficient, first of all because heat production in more intensively used rooms is far higher (greater activity, light, and machines means more heat). Secondly, combating humidity often proves difficult in regions with high groundwater levels, where building underground essentially amounts to building underwater, resulting in higher levels of atmospheric humidity.

Box-within-a-box

This is a structural solution available for problems both of humidity and of ventilation. Instead of using earth-retaining walls directly as insulated construction walls, a broadened cavity is fashioned between the construction wall and floor and the actual building. The construction of the box-within-a-box structure is somewhat less critical, as groundwater seeping in through the outer walls does not penetrate directly into the building itself. Humidity, naturally, has to be removed by ventilation. The box-within-a-box construction is not only structurally favourable; it also makes all of the ingredients necessary for a pleasant underground interior climate more attainable. If the exterior box is well insulated, the surrounding earth remains cool in summer and relatively warm in winter. Of course, this can also be realised without the box-within-a-box construction; the construction walls of a given structure simply have to be well insulated. The stable temperatures of the ground can then be used to cool or heat the space economically. This can be achieved by a channel in the ground supplying fresh outside air. In both warmer and cooler months, the air takes on the temperature of the ground, so that cooling or heating air requires less energy. This system can serve as the basis for natural underground ventilation.

Underground ventilation

Introducing natural ventilation into underground buildings is difficult, however, since the wind does not blow directly at the building. Somehow, the wind must be made to enter. In other words, it must be guided downwards. Differences in air pressure within the building are required to make the wind stream through the complex and ensure the necessary exchange of air. In this way, unpleasant smells – one of the causes of an unpleasant feeling in a building – are dispelled, and cool air can absorb excess heat.

Historic examples of such systems of natural ventilation include the famous wind towers, or *badgirs*, used in Pakistan. Warm wind is diverted into the towers, which are built of thick stone, via wind scoops. The stone body absorbs heat from the wind; the wind cools down and therefore descends. Once inside, the cool wind absorbs heat generated within the building, and then rises and leaves the building, generally via the courtyard, which may

Limburg Archives
Maastricht,
the Netherlands
RDG/Marc van Roosmalen

241

Box-within-a-box
construction

be covered. This thermal draught can be stimulated in contemporary underground buildings by capping the court-yard with glass. Given the necessity of daylight in underground buildings, such glazed space is essential, anyway. It is warmer directly under the glass than in the lower portions of an underground building, and this creates more powerful wind circulation.

Double skin

To distribute fresh, cool air in an underground building, an atrium or the broadened cavity of the box-within-a-box can be used. This construction then works as a sort of underground double skin. Users can admit fresh air by opening windows! In a subterranean situation, that is an incredible fact, and one that increases the users' control of the interior climate. Air quality must, naturally, be very good. In the case of a box-within-a-box construction, this means that too much humidity, which promotes the formation of fungus in the cavity, must be prevented. This requires a room that is at once structurally sealed and extremely well ventilated. Apart from that, any harm-ful radon coming from the earth must be avoided and the box must be closed. Of course, if windows open the shell of the building to look out onto a broadened cavity, this space should also constitute a striking architectonic element. Views of a closed, sombre concrete wall would only serve to confirm the impression of being shut in. One option is an underground version of the facade devised by the American agency, SITE, for Best Department Stores, with a tropical garden laid out between double glass plates.

Plenty of green – not only in the cavity or the atrium, but also in the rooms themselves – also improves interior climate considerably. Most people like to work in an environment with plenty of plants, perhaps because it gives

242

THE HOLE IN THE WORLD

Driving east from the centre of the port of Den Helder, we find a rural landscape that transports us into another world. A herd of white ponies, manes flying, races up the moss and fern-covered hills. The moving scene is almost like a miniature Devon, or Ireland, set in the middle of the Netherlands. In fact, this idyll is an inland dune area, full of bunkers erected by the Germans as part of the Atlantic Wall.

'De Nollen', as the area is referred to, was leased in 1981 to an artist named R.W. van de Wint, who has created his life's work here. The fourteen hectare site not only offers him the freedom to dig out pools and hollows, raise hills and manipulate nature, but more importantly to devise and build constructions, make and exhibit sculptures and transform the bunkers into a site for wall paintings.

Aether II is a corten steel gate and dome placed on top of one of the bunkers. It is painted in gradated shades, beginning with cobalt blue and progressing to white at its apex, a divinely beautiful work of art that is forever unfinished. Van de Wint's paintings, composed of multiple layers, remain in interim stages

permanently. As the years pass, he changes his mind and starts all over again using new colour schemes.

One spectacular work involves a subterranean passageway. Lit on both sides by nightlights, it is impossible to tell where it ends. It is the archetype of the underground space: here you find yourself in pitch-blackness, the light too feeble to offer any sense of size or direction. Our sole point of reference is a blue light bulb at the end of the passage, beyond which we turn left to follow another corridor, lit by nightlights. Perhaps the mirrors and the candles are not actually where we had thought. Who knows? Now, the uneven grade creates uncer-tainty as well. The passageway at right angles splits into two here. Higher and to the left, we are led to one of a pair of thatched cupolas, visible from without. It is a relief to be above ground again, in this recognisable shape. The inside is finished with whitewashed clay and a prism is suspended from above, refracting sunlight and projecting it onto twenty different places in the room. Van de Wint excels at playing with chiaroscuro.

the impression of being outdoors. Plants also have a regulatory effect on atmospheric humidity, a great advantage in an underground environment, with its tendency toward humidity. They also absorb dust and retain chemical elements such as formaldehyde and ammonia.

Light and sound

Both cavity and atrium need to be well-sealed with glass at the top. On the one hand, this improves thermal draught, as described above. On the other, it enables daylight to penetrate deep into the underground space. Despite the impossibility of creating a direct view, this provides users with the impression of there being 'an outside'. In achieving a pleasant atmosphere, sound plays a similar role to that of daylight. Audible noises from outside counteract the feeling of being shut in. It is not presently possible to allow natural outside noises to penetrate into underground buildings, which means the risk of an acoustically dead and therefore dismal atmosphere. Bringing weather and traffic noises inside is practically impossible and would lead, in any case, to a tangibly artificial environment. It is better to permit more background noise than in aboveground buildings and to use less sound-absorbent materials. An increase in sound levels of about 5 decibels is desirable. Such sounds can be voices in conversation (so long as they cannot be understood), or can come from other activities in the complex, or mechanical equipment.

Buddy building

Proper insulation of underground functional rooms, which prevents excessive heating of the surrounding earth, is also advantageous, but not only for climatising underground complexes. Air that is pre-cooled or pre-heated by

243

The other cupola is entitled 'The Hole in the World'. A hole in the floor leads several metres downward into the depths and projects the heavens, on the other side of the world, onto a screen.
The hole offers no escape – we are trapped. The walls of the round construction continue without interruption: infinity. We will have to retrace our steps along the entire route. From light to darkness and back to light again, the hole in our world.

the earth body can be used in aboveground sections. Such a link between underground and aboveground buildings is desirable for several reasons. First of all for the sake of the possible exchange of heat and cold. A 'buddy building' also offers advantages from a technical and structural point of view, since it is difficult to install machinery in underground buildings. In the extension of the Andersson Elffers Felix office, in Utrecht, Mecanoo solved the problem elegantly by housing the air treatment plant in a wall unit. Mecanoo enjoyed an advantage, however, in that the underground space accommodated primarily conference rooms, which present relatively few problems with heat. Furthermore, the extension is in, or should we say under, the back garden. The air sucked inside is therefore relatively clean. In most urban environments, things are far more difficult. The air at street level is too polluted to feed into the building unfiltered, so fresh outside air has to be obtained from elsewhere. Moreover, combustion gases may not be emitted at street level, but must be expelled above the highest building in the vicinity. The roof of an aboveground buddy building can be used for both taking in fresh air and for discharging exhausted air.

Guaranteed interior climate

Machinery can also be used more efficiently with a building that lies both under and above ground. On the one hand, since heating and cooling requirements for underground and aboveground will not be entirely synchronised, heat and cool can be exchanged. On the other hand, a fairly complicated installation will be needed for any underground building. No matter how ingenious a system for generating natural ventilation, a pleasant interior climate underground cannot be guaranteed by natural means alone. If use is made of wind pressure – as with the badgirs in Pakistan – then the system is ineffective when the wind dies down, while systems based on thermal draught require temperature differences. A combination of both systems is slightly safer, but nevertheless cannot guarantee the ventilation levels required by legislation all year round. Climate control systems therefore need to combine the mechanical supply and discharge of air with natural ventilation and an installation that can step in when it threatens to become too warm, too cold or too stuffy. This seems to involve double measures, but it prevents buildings from failing to operate optimally in periods of extremely hot or cold weather.

When determining the dimensioning of such installations, generation of a too even climate is to be avoided. Excessively stable temperature and atmospheric humidity make people extremely lethargic. Installations must provide slight variations, as with natural ventilation, which generates variations as a matter of course. Peter Luscuere, professor of Mechanical Engineering at the Technical University of Delft, once spoke of a machine with a tick. It permits climatic fluctuations – within the margins of what is perceived as pleasant, of course.

Buildings like icebergs

When aboveground buildings are linked to those underground, the resulting structures are like icebergs, with their larger parts below the surface. Functions other than storage (e.g., the Limburg Archives and the Zeeland Archives) and car parks should be seriously considered. Conference rooms and auditoria, as the wonderful examples in this book clearly illustrate, are possible. Sports facilities, cinemas and shops can also be accommodated. Spaces needing little or no daylight can be installed perfectly well and quite 'healthily' underground. In principle, comfort requirements do not differ from those in aboveground versions of the same functions. Sound insulation, required for cinemas, music venues and auditoria, is easier to realise underground, thanks to the body of the earth. Classrooms and offices can also be tucked away under ground level. For such locations, however, high demands are generally made in the area of comfort. If they are housed underground, some degree of compensation must be provided.

Extra stimulus

Certainly, underground buildings have to be different from 'normal' ones. Subterranean construction is not simply a question of building an aboveground building below ground. Although comfort requirements may be largely the same, they are more difficult to realise. The environment is actually not people-friendly. First of all, therefore, all facets generally perceived as characterising comfort must be included in designs at a high level. There has to be as much daylight and natural ventilation as possible, with excellent air quality. Sound levels must correspond with the building's function, with enough background noise admitted to compensate for the lack of natural outside noise. And, finally, there must be plenty of plants, large open rooms, friendly and restful colours and visual landmarks. If these awkward preconditions are complied with, then extraordinary spaces can be created, in which people will find it quite pleasant to work and engage in leisure activities. Being underground can then be experienced as an extra stimulus instead of a mere nuisance.

But is building underground also energy-efficient? When potential climate problems are solved below ground with machines alone, then such buildings are probably less economical than ordinary ones, simply because construction itself uses far more energy than for ordinary aboveground buildings, and because, in addition to normal installations, heavy-duty dehumidifiers are also necessary. If, however, optimal advantage is taken of the stable, cool environment and heat from the building is therefore prevented from 'polluting' the earth, then considerable energy savings can be generated.

SOFT AND HAIRY HOUSE
Tsukuba City Ushida-Findlay Partnership

TWO HOUSING PROJECTS

NINE HOUSES

Dietikon Peter Vetsch

With a little imagination, one could almost believe that this artificial landscape in Switzerland, designed by Peter Vetsch, was happily inhabited by a strange, but friendly people. Although clearly manufactured by human hands, his 'Nine Houses' are incorporated entirely into the rural environment. In Japan, the 'Soft and Hairy House' was fitted into a more urban landscape. The architects, Ushida-Findlay, approach the house as a microcosm of the city.

Soft and Hairy House

Salvador Dalí's remark that the architecture of the future would be soft and hairy inspired the Japanese-Scottish architects partnership of Eisaku Ushida and Kathryn Findlay to design a surrealistic house. Their clients wanted the local community of Tsukuba City, not far from Tokyo, to communicate the message that we must treat the environment gently. Its hairiness takes the form of the plants located on the roof, where vegetation is left to its own devices and is intended to resemble the wild and tangled site before it was built on. The roof hence implies spontaneous, natural growth in response to Japanese regimentation.

The soft part of the Soft and Hairy House is tangible in its undulating forms and use of materials. The more intimate rooms are enveloped as though within protective capsules, while the house itself folds around an inner courtyard. The height of surrealism is its blue, egg-shaped bathroom, which, as in other houses by these architects, is at the home's centre. With such unconventional forms, the designer has to be creative in applying materials. The egg is 'sprinkled' with glass discs to temper incoming light. Entirely in harmony with the soft and hairy theme are the walls, clad with canvas, while a door is covered with fur, both meant for leaning and sitting against.

248

Soft and Hairy House
Cross-section and
longitudinal section

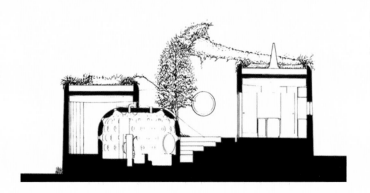

Soft and Hairy House

Roof and ground floor
plans

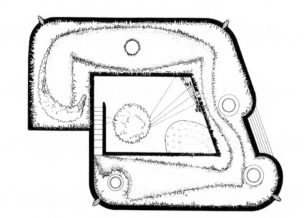

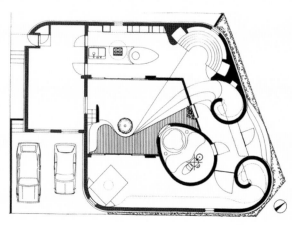

SOFT AND HAIRY HOUSE

Function **home**

Address **Tsukuba City, Japan**

Construction volume **500 m³**

Floor surface **175 m²**

Depth **0 metres**

Number of levels underground **1**

Design **1994**

Construction **1994**

Architects **Ushida-Findlay Partnership, Tokyo**

250

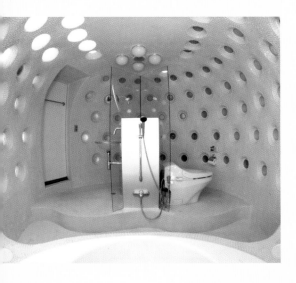

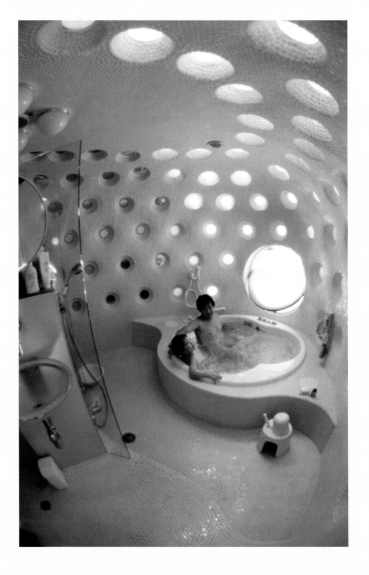

Nine Houses

Swiss architect Peter Vetsch went a step further than Ushida-Findlay in his Nine Houses complex, where he made no distinction whatsoever between floors, walls and roof. The earth-covered housing complex is situated in a hilly area, and blends effortlessly into its surroundings. The houses are clustered around a lake and scattered over a U-shaped hill. Their organic construction consists of shotcrete, with a 25-centimetre layer of polymer bitumen and recycled glass foam on top. Access to the houses is at the sides, entirely out of sight, to the benefit of their free forms. Size is variable, from four to seven rooms, with living rooms facing south and bedrooms north. Interior rooms such as kitchens and bathrooms are illuminated by domed skylights. The form of the hill makes it possible for each home to have an outdoor space that is entirely out of sight of its neighbours, with underground garages and cellars. Vetsch derived his organic forms from nature, while the burrowing behaviour of animals inspired the interior designs.

252

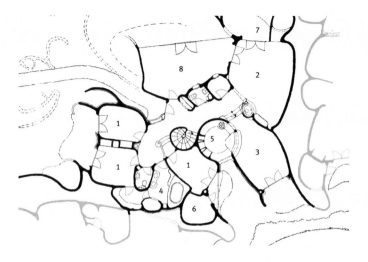

Nine Houses

1 Bedroom

2 Living room

3 Dining room

4 Bathroom

5 Kitchen

6 Storage

7 Terrace

8 Winter garden

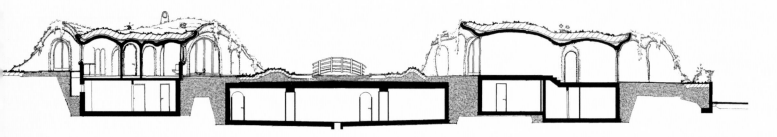

Nine Houses

Section

NINE HOUSES

Function **homes**

Address **Dietikon, Switzerland**

Construction volume **600 m³-2,200 m³**

per house

Floor surface **60 m²-200 m² per house**

Depth **2.5 metres**

Number of levels underground **2**

Design **1993**

Construction **1993**

Architect **Peter Vetsch, Dietikon**

TWO LIBRARIES

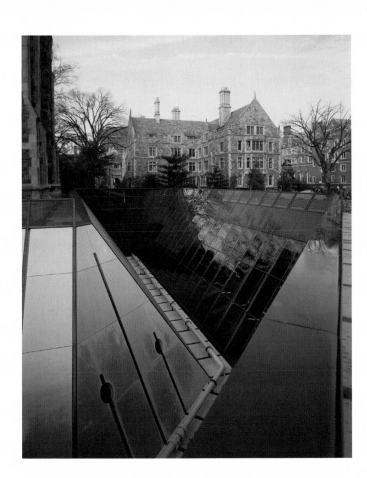

LAW FACULTY LIBRARY, UNIVERSITY OF MICHIGAN

Ann Arbor Gunnar Birkerts & Associates

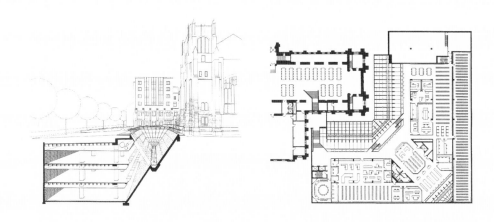

Law Faculty library

Section and plan

LAW FACULTY LIBRARY

Function **extension to Law Faculty library**

Address **Ann Arbor, Michigan, United**

States of America

Floor surface **8,000 m²**

Depth **12 metres**

Number of levels underground **3**

Construction time **3 years**

Design **1976-1979**

Construction **1978-1981**

Client **University of Michigan**

Architects **Gunnar Birkerts & Associates,**

Michigan

Architect Gunnar Birkerts, originally from Latvia, has several underground projects to his credit, chiefly extensions of North American campuses. Birkerts says: 'It is my intention to go underground without degrading the building's users, who can sit or move about in the space with no oppressive sense of burial in a remote sub-basement.' The library of the Law Faculty in Ann Arbor, extended by Birkerts in the 1970s, folds itself around the contours of the rectangular superstructure. The more recent Marriott Library, in Salt Lake City, also wraps around the original library, but now in response to its surroundings, and with a more playful contour.

Law Faculty library, University of Michigan, Ann Arbor

An L-shaped extension has been added to the original library, a detached, neo-Gothic building from the 1920s. Between it and the new underground building, a V-shaped glass trench has been constructed, a sort of glass moat. The daylight penetrating within is carried by a slanted wall – an extended side of the V – to three underlying storeys. This sloping wall, of pale sandstone, is placed at such an angle that light entering from above falls horizontally into each storey. Birkerts has fitted the posts of the light trench with an ingenious system of mirrors, which not only intensifies the daylight, but also transport an outside view deep into the building. This makes the V-shaped light-catcher the one structured element of the construction, emphasised by an atrium, keeping the three storeys at a distance. From the balconies, where balustrades have been built out into workstations, there is a wonderful view of the characteristic main building. From outside, a skylight is also visible. At the extreme of the upright letter 'L' is a smaller, triangular skylight, giving some notion of the size of the underground building from outside. This skylight also prevents any disturbing backlight. Due partly to the use of natural light and its compact construction, this underground extension saves 20% on energy consumption, when compared to an aboveground building.

MARRIOTT LIBRARY, UNIVERSITY OF UTAH

Salt Lake City Gunnar Birkerts & Associates

The original library building on the University of Utah campus is distributed through five storeys. A columnar grid of approximately eight by eight metres gives this square box a clear structure. The new underground building folds itself around three sides of the building, apparently at random, but actually in such a way that the original grid could be continued, emphasising cohesion between old and new. Although, strictly speaking, the existing building has only one underground floor, the level differences in the surroundings mean that visitors enter on the first floor, hence perceiving two storeys as being underground. The library extension also has a subterranean and an aboveground storey. But because the roof was constructed as an elevated ground level with terraces, the building is virtually invisible. The new building is subordinate to the landscape and only shows itself in the amorphous – but not too obvious – excavations: the five large courtyards which provide study areas with daylight and views. Three of these separate the old building from the new, with wide connection zones in between. Unlike the library in Ann Arbor, the mass of craggy mountains in the background gives the courtyards a natural look.

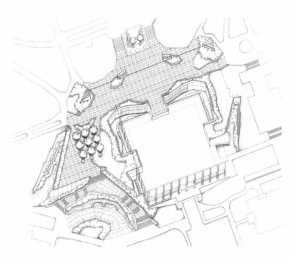

MARRIOTT LIBRARY

Function	**extension to Marriott Library**
Address	**Salt Lake City, Utah, United States of America**
Floor surface	**1,600 m²**
Depth	**4 metres**
Number of levels underground	**2**
Construction time	**3 years**
Design	**1992**
Construction	**1994-1996**
Client	**University of Utah**
Architects	**Gunnar Birkerts & Associates, Michigan**

Marriott Library **261**

Axonometric projection
and plan
1 Courtyard
2 Entrance
3 Classrooms

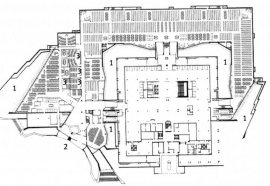

Acknowledgements

Ernst von Meijenfeldt

For most of my life, I have been fascinated by underground building. That fascination is primarily about connections, both with the environment and with nature. Also, I think it's wonderful to create space by subtraction – excavating – rather than by addition – enclosing. Of course, I have been regularly laughed at over the past 21 years. 'Building underground? Great. But what's the point? It's really rather fringe, isn't it?' In addition to those critics, however, there were also the allies, those who helped to lead the way towards to this book. I recall them with fondness.

During my early years of study in Delft, inspiring encounters with the works of architects like Wright, Soleri, Le Corbusier, Barragan, the Smithsons, Goff, Morgan and Ambasz, left a lasting impression. It seemed to me that, for them, building under ground was not a formula for attaining a connection with nature. It is simply one architectural tool available for concretising that relationship.

Jeroen Trimbos was my principal ally during those early years. I thank him for the great adventures and expeditions we undertook to China and North America. It was with him that I made my first underground designs: noise barrier homes in Hardegarijp and an underground extension to the town hall of Steenwijk, both in the Netherlands. In 1986, together with Subhan van Lohuizen, Jeroen and I established the Nova Terra Foundation, following in the footsteps of the Underground Space Center in Minneapolis. Our continuous exchange with John Carmody and Ray Sterling meant a lot to us. For the first time, people other than engineers were involved in the discipline: architects, urban developers and other designers. This led, in 1992, to a big conference in Delft, with major contributions from, among others, Arthur Quarmby, Sindney Baggs and Hans Hollein.

After the Centrum Ondergronds Bouwen COB was set up, the development of subterranean structure in the Netherlands accelerated at lightning speed. In 1998, under my supervision, a study of the spatial aspects of underground building began (the O-100 study). In the space of two years, ten sub-disciplines were explored and analysed: Urban Development & Landscape, Architecture, Movement, Technology, Perception, Intuitive Perception, Literature Study, Project Analysis, Imagination and Process. A preparatory study was also carried out for a number of these partial projects. Visions and ideas were developed by OMA and MVRDV, in particular, which were then explored and visualised in highly creative ways. My thanks to all research teams and especially to project leaders Wim Snelders, Floris Alkemade, Peter Lüthi, Peter Blesgraaf, Renz van Luxemburg, Heather Griffioen-Young, Peter Jonquière, Jeroen Trimbos and Rob van de Krogt.

To Mari Baauw, my thanks for his unfailing support in terms of both content and organisation. Also indispensable were COB managers Hans Kuiper and Mascha Sanders, and their respective successors, Han Admiraal and Marjolijn Bakker. Without them, this project would never have got off the ground. Working for and with them has been an inspiring and pleasant privilege.

Below Ground Level was produced on the basis of the extensive material generated by the O-100 study. Translating it into a manageable book without losing the essential content has been an intriguing and inspiring experience. For that, I thank all the authors and all of the architectural agencies who cooperated so unselfishly. It has been a great privilege to be able, finally, to commit my fascination to paper in the form of words and images. I would also like to thank the personnel at my agency. By taking as much work off my hands as possible, they enabled me to devote more time to this project. My special thanks to Marit Geluk. Her thoroughness and sense of humour enriched this book. Our collaboration over the past eighteen months, during which this book was produced, is very precious to me.

Finally, my thanks to my wife, Zizi Lievers. She not only gave me the freedom and support to finish this book, but her critical abilities were a continual incentive to keep to the essence. She is my living 'hidden space', the woman of my heart.

Ernst von Meijenfeldt
Amsterdam, 18 April 2002

Illustration Credits

All efforts have been made to identify the interested parties. Anyone wishing to assert his or her rights is kindly requested to contact V+K Publishing.

ADAGP Michel Denance 239, 240
ADAGP George Fessy 238
O. Alamany & E. Vicens/CORBIS 18
Emilio Ambasz 16, 44-49
Tadao Ando 22
Arends, 1997 214
Ballast Nedam 210-211
Dave Barttruff CORBIS 23
Henni van Beek 243
Bettman/CORBIS 179
Gunnar Birkerts 260
Jocelyne van den Bossche 78-79
Julian Calder/CORBIS 23
John Carmody 231, 233
Peter Cook/VIEW 142
Cruz en Ortiz 53, 54
Richard Davies 17, 134, 150, 152-154
Guus Dubbelman/Frank Goor 41-43
Peter Durant (Arcblue) 80, 81
Erich Meyer 100
Gisela Erlacher/ARCAID 151, 156, 157
Collectie Filmmuseum 15, 209
Kees Franssen, HBG Civiel 216, 217
A. Furudate/Kozlowski/Guy Jordan 19
A. Furudate/Kozlowski/Guy Jordan 19
Geo Informatiecentrum Amsterdam 40
Dennis Gilbert (VIEW) 74-77
Darrell Gulin/CORBIS 93
Roland Halbe 20, 175
COB underground architecture manual, 1997, 212 margin
Hans Werleman 97, 107
Pentti Harala Ky 186, 188, 189, 191
Rob 't Hart 162, 187, 192, 193, back cover
Thomas A. Heinz/CORBIS 13

Hubert-Jan Henket Architecten 238
S. Henselmans 94
Hiroshi Ueda 99
Hans Hollein 21
Jaap Huisman 95
Timothy Hursley 3
Timothy Hursley 176, 256-259
Wolfgang Kaehler/CORBIS 91
Katsuhisha Kida 235, 246, 249-251
Peter Vetsch 247
Ken Kirkwood 133
Luuk Kramer 7, 96
Kuiper compagnons 101
Michael S. Lewis/CORBIS 13
Jannes Linders 116,-121, 201, 224-229
Misuo Matsuoka 143
Medilux 173
Ernst von Meijenfeldt 171, 174, 231, 237
James Morris 165
David Muench/CORBIS 92
MVRDV 50, 62-67
Monica Nicoliek 17
Robert Oerlemans 105, 241
OMA 212
Norbert van Onna 135, 146, 147, 149
Gerrit Oorthuys 56, 57
Richard Bryant 100
Christian Richters cover, 4, 10, 11, 24-39, 53, 89, 98, 108-110, 112-115, 139, 159, 160, 169, 218-221, 223
RMN/Caroline Rose 1, 111
Tom de Rooij 58
Galen Rowell/CORBIS 92
David Samuel Robbins/CORBIS 93
SBR, 1995 207
Scagliola/Bakker 55
Paul A. Souders/CORBIS 103
Speltdoorn 167
James Stoke 88, 123, 128, 129
Jussi Tiainen 180, 181, 183, 184, 185
Jeroen Trimbos 18

Hiroshi Ueda 143
From: Earth Sheltered housing design 8
Van Hillo Verschaeren Architecten 138
Peter Vetsch 234, 252-255
Ger van der Vlugt 106
Karl Weatherly 148
Takashi Yamaguchi & Associates, Masatoshi Okumura, Kaori Ichikawa 122, 124, 125, 127
Nigel Young 2, 68-70, 72, 73, 96, 131, 132
Kim Zwarts 163, 194, 195, 197, 198

263

With thanks to

Han Admiraal, Agence Dominique Perrault, Floris Alkemade, Emilio Ambasz, Tadao Ando, Atelier Hans Hollein, Atelier Peichl, Mari Baauw, Ballast Nedam, Jan Benthem, Bezoekerscentrum de Hoep, Gunnar Birkerts, Busmann & Haberer Architecten, John Carmody, Carrousel du Louvre, Jo Crepain, Cruz & Ortiz, David Chipperfield Architects, Norman Foster, Massimiliano Fuksas, Galeries Lafayette, Hubert-Jan Henket, het Zeeuws Archief, Kees van der Hoeven, Francine Houben, Hyvämäki-Karhunen-Parkkinen Architects, Ian Ritchie Architects, Jestico + Whiles, Kölner Philharmonie, Jaqueline van Koningsbruggen, Marc Labadie, Zizi Lievers, Paul Litjens, Johan Matser Projectontwikkeling bv, John McAslan + Partners, Murphy/Jahn, Museum Beelden aan Zee, Gerrit Oorthuys, Penitentiaire Inrichting Breda, Wim Quist, Marc van Roosmalen, Rutten Communicatie en Advies, Claudio Silvestrin Architects, Stichting de Nollen, Jeroen Trimbos, Peter Vetsch, Takashi Yamaguchi, Zwarts & Jansma Architecten

Colophon

Concept

Ernst von Meijenfeldt, Marit Geluk, Architecten-en Ontwerpbureau von Meijenfeldt, Amsterdam, the Netherlands

Editor

Ernst von Meijenfeldt

Illustration editor

Marit Geluk

Interviews

Ernst von Meijenfeldt

Project descriptions

Marit Geluk, Ernst von Meijenfeldt

Final editing of the Dutch edition and elaboration of interviews

Jacco Hogeweg, Sabel communicatie, Utrecht, the Netherlands

English translation

Roz Vatter-Buck, Biran, France

Copy editing of the English edition

Ian Pepper, Berlin, Germany

Design

Cees de Jong, Josine Overduin, Jan Johan ter Poorten, V+K Design, Blaricum, the Netherlands

Lithography and printing

Snoeck-Ducaju & Zoon bv, Gent, Belgium

Publicity

Ellen ten Broecke, Indigo, Rotterdam, the Netherlands

Commissioned by

Han Admiraal, Marjolijn Bakker, Gisela van Blokland, Wendy Kooijmans, Mascha Sanders, Centrum Ondergronds Bouwen, Gouda, the Netherlands

This publication is based on the study 'Ondergrondse Ruimte', carried out between 1998 and 2000, commissioned by the Centrum Ondergronds Bouwen in Gouda, the Netherlands. This research, referred to as the O100 study, was carried out under the supervision of Ernst von Meijenfeldt, Chairman, and Mari Baauw, Secretary. Ten part reports served as the foundation for the following chapters:

Chapter 2

O101 *Omgeving – stedenbouw en landschap* Wim Snelders, Ballast Nedam Engineering, Amstelveen; Winy Maas, MVRDV, Rotterdam

Chapter 3

O102 *Architectuur* Floris Alkemade, Office for Metropolitan Architecture, Rotterdam

Chapter 5

O103 *Beweging* Peter Lüthi, Department of Architecture, Delft Technical University
O105 *Waarnemen* Renz van Luxemburg, Centre for Architectural Research, Institute of Applied Scientific Research – Eindhoven Technical University
O106 *Intuïtief waarnemen* Heather Griffioen-Young, Institute of Applied Scientific Research – Human Factors Research Institute, Soesterberg; Sander Korz, Eysink Smeets & Etman, The Hague

Chapter 6

O104 *Techniek* Peter Blesgraaf, Blesgraaf Construction and Environmental Agency, Rijswijk; Ed Smienk, ABT, Arnhem

General

O110 *Literatuurstudie* Peter Jonquière; Zandvoort Ordening & Advies, Utrecht
O120 *Projectanalyse* Jeroen Trimbos, PAM Consultants, Den Haag; Jaap Modder, NIROV, Den Haag; Peter Jonquière, Zandvoort Ordening & Advies, Utrecht
O130 *Verbeelding* Jeroen Trimbos, PAM Consultants, Den Haag
O140 *Proces* Rob van der Krogt, DHV Milieu en Infrastructuur, Amersfoort

264